MW00648872

MASS & ADORATION COMPANION

Vinny Flynn
& Erin Flynn

TAN Books
Charlotte, North Carolina

"Even if all the physical hunger of the world were satisfied, even if everyone who is hungry were fed by his or her own labor or by the generosity of others, the deepest hunger of man would still exist. . . .

"Therefore, I say, 'Come, all of you, to Christ. He is the bread of life. Come to Christ and you will never be hungry again.'"

—Pope St. John Paul II[1]

DEDICATION

For all of our beloved priests, who,
each day, rend the veil of heaven and
give to us the greatest gift of our lives
here on earth—the Holy Eucharist

CONTENTS

The Liturgy of the Eucharist

Communion Prayers

Thanksgiving Prayers

Eucharistic Adoration

Adoration Prayers

Prayers for Various Occasions

Prayers, Litanies, and Novenas

INTRODUCTION

I HAVE a confession to make. When I asked my daughter Erin to begin compiling these prayers, it wasn't primarily with you in mind. I wanted it for myself. And since Erin and I have often shared our favorite prayers, I knew she would want it too.

So this little book is not just a random collection of prayers. And it's not a "historical" book presenting an arrangement of traditional Catholic prayers written throughout the ages. There are many such books, and they serve their purpose well.

But that wasn't our intent. What we have put together is a careful, loving selection of prayers—some old, some new—that are especially meaningful and fruitful for us so that we wouldn't merely be spectators during Mass, wouldn't merely be reciting prayers and responses, but would be fully present and actively involved through specific prayers that would help us really enter in, speaking to God and to Our Lady, person-to-person, from our hearts.

With this in mind, we found some prayers that seemed so perfectly expressed that we have presented them here in their entirety. Others are brief excerpts of longer prayers. Still others are original prayers that we composed ourselves, or adaptations in which we tried to capture, in simple prayer, the beautiful insights we found in Scripture, the teachings of the Church, and the writings of some of our great saints and popes.

Personalized Prayer

Many years ago, I was greatly moved by the way St. Faustina talked with God. She had come to realize that God wants a relationship with each of us that is completely real and personal. So she developed a natural way of praying to God in the most personal, loving, and intimate language imaginable—so much so that it shocked and angered others in her community who demanded to know who she thought she was to talk to God that way.

It struck me that she knew who she was: she was "Daddy's little girl," and that's who He had created her to be.

Since then, in my own prayer life, I have gradually moved away from using any ways of praying that seem too formal, distant, or artificial—ways that don't simply and honestly express what I'm feeling and experiencing in the here and now of my life, ways that don't draw me into a deeper relationship with the God who loves me.

When I recite traditional prayers with others during the Holy Mass or other group situations, I pray them as they are written, for the sake of unity, but in my private prayer moments, when it's just me and God, I pray them in the way that is most real and natural to me.

You're the Editor

This became our guiding principle as we selected, edited, adapted, updated, wrote, or rewrote the prayers you'll find here. Now that we've compiled and arranged them, we're delighted to share them with you, and I encourage you to make this book your own so that it may draw you deeper and deeper into your own, unique, one-on-One relationship with God.

Don't be locked in by the exact wording of the prayers, but please feel free to make whatever changes seem most natural for you. (I pray some of these prayers differently every day.)

If a change in the wording of a particular prayer would help you pray it in a more meaningful way, then grab your pen and do it. Let the printed prayers be simply a starting point for your prayer—a framework that will inspire you to enter into your own private conversation with the Lord and with Our Lady.

After some sections, we have included blank pages for you to fill with your favorite prayers. You can write them right on the page or type them on a piece of paper and glue them in. If a particular prayer in the book just isn't meaningful to you, then paste a different prayer over it. Remember, it's your book, so use it in whatever way will help you draw closer to the Lord. Don't be afraid to put a star by certain prayers, draw boxes around them, circle or underline parts that are particularly meaningful, use a highlighter, or add bookmarks and prayercards—whatever will help you to personalize your prayer.

HEART TO HEART

St. Therese wrote that prayer is above all "a surge of the heart toward God."[2] That doesn't mean that we should never use words to pray, but it does mean that true prayer is always an expression of personal relationship in which your heart reaches toward the Heart of God.

God delights in the uniqueness of each of His children. He treasures the you He created, and He wants a relationship with you that's different from His relationship with anyone else. So when you pray to Him, it's important to use words that help you lift your mind and heart to Him in a real expression of that personal relationship.

We offer this book to you, then, as a beginning, not an end, a draft to be finished by you, so that your prayer will become truly *your* prayer, your heart-to-Heart conversation with the Lord.

May it bless you!

Vinny Flynn

NOTE

We have done our best to determine and cite the original sources for the prayers and quotes included here. Some citations are provided in the text itself; others are referenced by footnote number in the notes section in the back of the book. But many of the prayers were compiled, updated, edited, or adapted from various secondary sources that do not contain any reference to the original source. Searching through old books and booklets, pamphlets, leaflets, prayer cards, and hundreds of websites and blogs, we often found many different versions of the same prayers, with no citations for any of them.

We have selected what we feel are the most powerful and inspiring of these prayers, and have included whatever source information we could find.

We have given most of the prayers specific titles to identify them and make them easier to find.

THE HOLY
SACRIFICE OF
THE MASS

———— ✦ ————

"Oh, what awesome mysteries
take place during Mass! . . .
One day we will know
what God is doing for us
in each Mass,
and what sort of gift
He is preparing in it for us.
Only His divine love
could permit that such a
gift be provided for us."

—St. Faustina, *Diary*, 914

PRAYERS
BEFORE MASS

"I will go in to the altar of God, the God of my joy!"

—*See Ps 43:4*

RECEIVE, O HOLY TRINITY

RECEIVE, O Holy Trinity, One God, this Holy Sacrifice of the Body and Blood of our Lord Jesus Christ, which I, Your unworthy servant, desire now to offer to Your Divine Majesty by the hands of this Your minister, with all the Sacrifices which have ever been or will be offered to You, in union with that most Holy Sacrifice offered by the same Christ our Lord at the Last Supper, and on the Altar of the Cross.

I offer it to You with the utmost affection and devotion, out of love for Your infinite goodness, and according to the intention of Jesus Christ and of His Church.

O God, almighty and merciful, grant us through this Holy Sacrifice, joy and peace, a holier life, the desire to die to self, grace and consolation of the Holy Spirit, and perseverance in good works.

In Union With All the Masses

LORD Jesus, through the Immaculate Heart of Mary, I offer myself in union with the once-for-all offering You made to the Father for my sins and the sins of the whole world.

Knowing that all the fruits of that eternal sacrifice on the cross are made present and available to us in each Eucharistic liturgy, I unite myself now with all the Masses being celebrated throughout the world. I ask You, Merciful Lord, to pour out upon me and my loved ones a drop of Your Precious Blood from each of these Masses to heal and sanctify us.

—Vinny Flynn

FOR SINNERS AND SOULS IN PURGATORY

ETERNAL Father, I offer You the Most Precious Blood of Your Divine Son, Jesus, in union with all the Masses said throughout the world today, for all the holy souls in Purgatory, for sinners everywhere, for sinners in the universal Church, for those in my own home and within my family.

—St. Gertrude[3]

AS I APPROACH YOUR BANQUET

I DRAW near, loving Lord, Jesus Christ, to the table of Your most delectable banquet in fear and trembling; for I am a sinner, relying not on my own merit, but trusting rather in Your mercy and goodness. I come with a heart and body defiled by many offenses, and a mind and tongue I have not guarded well.

Therefore, O loving God, O awesome Majesty, I, in my misery and caught in snares, turn to You the fount of mercy, hastening to You for healing, flying to You for protection; I would fear to draw near You as Judge, but long to have You as Savior.

To You, O Lord, I display my wounds, to You I uncover my shame. I am aware of my many and great sins, and they fill me with fear, but I hope in Your mercies, for they cannot be numbered.

Look upon me, then, with eyes of mercy, Lord Jesus Christ, eternal King, God and Man, crucified for mankind. Hear me, for my hope is in You; have mercy on me, full of miseries and sins, You, who will never cease to let the fountain of compassion flow.

Hail, O Saving Victim, offered for me and for all humanity on the wood of the Cross. Hail, O noble and precious Blood, flowing from the wounds of Jesus Christ, my crucified Lord, and washing away the sins of all the world.

Remember, Lord, Your creature, whom You redeemed by Your Blood. I repent of my sins, and I desire to put right what I have done. Take from me, therefore, most merciful Father, all my iniquities and sins, so that, purified in mind and body, I may worthily taste the Holy of Holies.

And grant that this sacred foretaste of Your Body and Blood which I, though unworthy, intend to receive, may be the remission of my sins, the perfect cleansing of my faults, the banishment of shameful thoughts, and the rebirth of holy desires. May it bring about the accomplishment of works most pleasing to You; and may it be for me a firm defense of body and soul against the snares of my enemies.

—Prayer of St. Ambrose

PRAYER TO ST. JOSEPH

O BLESSED Joseph, to whom it was given not only to see and to hear that God Whom many kings longed to see, and saw not, to hear, and heard not; but also to carry Him in your arms, to embrace Him, to clothe Him, and guard and defend Him, pray for me that I may unite myself completely with Him during this Holy Mass, worshipping Him in gratitude and joy.

O God, who have given us a royal priesthood, we beseech You, that as Blessed Joseph was found worthy to touch with his hands, and to bear in his arms, Your only-begotten Son, born of the Virgin Mary, so may we be made fit, by cleanness of heart and blamelessness of life, to approach Your holy altar.

May we, this day, with reverent devotion, partake of the Sacred Body and Blood of Your Only-begotten Son, and may we be accounted worthy of receiving an everlasting reward in the world to come.

THAT I MAY BE WORTHY

WHO can worthily be present at this sacrifice, unless You, O God, make him worthy? I know, Lord (truly I know and humbly confess to Your loving kindness) that, because of my numberless sins and negligences, I am unworthy to approach so great a mystery.

But I also know (and truly believe in my heart and confess with my tongue) that You can make me worthy, You who alone can make clean those who are unclean, and make sinners become just and holy. By this Your almighty power I ask You, Lord, to grant that I, a sinner, may enter into this sacrifice with awe and reverence, with purity of heart and true repentance, with spiritual gladness and heavenly joy. May my mind feel the sweetness of Your most blessed presence, and the love of Your holy angels keeping watch around me.

—Adapted from a Prayer of St. Ambrose

Mass Intentions

ETERNAL Father, I unite myself with the intentions and affections of Our Lady of Sorrows on Calvary, and I offer to You the sacrifice that your beloved Son Jesus made of Himself upon the cross, and now renews upon this holy altar.

I make this offering:

To adore You and give You the honor that is due to You, confessing Your supreme dominion over all things, and the absolute dependence of everything upon You, who are our sole and our last end;

To thank You for the countless benefits that I have received;

To appease Your justice, aroused against us by so many sins, and to make satisfaction for them;

To implore grace for myself, for _____, for all afflicted and sorrowing, for poor sinners, for all the world, and for the holy souls in purgatory.

—Adapted from a Prayer by Pope St. Pius X,
Acta Sanctae Sedis, July 8, 1904

I Leave Behind the World

MOST Holy Trinity, Father, Son, and Holy Spirit, I leave behind the world for a time and enter into this Sacred space: to worship You, to give You thanks, to allow You, in Your great kindness, to restore me—You who continually make all things new.

If this space helps lift my mind, my soul, to eternal realities, I praise You, and give thanks for those who labored to make it so. If not, O Lord, no matter. I close my eyes and revel in the reality of Your beauty. What You will accomplish here, regardless of man's indifference, is the most sublime thing on earth. The most beautiful. The most sacred. The highest good. Draw me in to this miraculous mystery of Your love.

I surrender to You all the distractions and worries that war within me. Help me to prepare, in my mind and heart, fertile ground for all the graces You will pour out during this Holy Mass. I repent of any sins, any ways I have turned away from You, and I ask for your healing mercy.

I pray in gratitude for Your priests here, for all priests, for the brothers and sisters who worship by my side, and for all those I hold in my heart. Bless each of them in their need, and draw them ever closer to you.

As I participate in this glorious encounter of heaven and earth, may I be filled with wonder and awe at the great mysteries unfolding before me. May I receive Holy Communion with reverence and love, and allow Your Presence within me to change me for the better. You who bless, You who heal, You who inspire; send me out, then, to do the same.

—Erin Flynn

My Prayers Before Mass

My Prayers Before Mass

"We go to heaven
when we go to Mass.
This is not merely a symbol,
not a metaphor, not a parable,
not a figure of speech. It is real. . . .
The Mass—and I mean
every single Mass—
is heaven on earth."

—Scott Hahn[4]

INTRODUCTORY RITES
AND THE LITURGY
OF THE WORD

*"You have come to Mount Zion,
to the city of the living God,
the heavenly Jerusalem."*

—Heb 12:22 NIV

THE PENITENTIAL ACT

*After the processional, the priest "calls upon the whole
community to take part in the Penitential Act . . ."*
—The General Instruction of the Roman Missal, no. 51

"Brethren (brothers and sisters) let us acknowledge our sins, and so prepare ourselves to celebrate the sacred mysteries."

*A brief pause for silence follows, during which you can
ask the Lord to bring to mind any sins or attachment to
sins, repent of them, and ask for forgiveness and healing.*

L ORD, send Your Holy Spirit to help me call to
mind any ways I have offended You. I repent
of all my sins, all my failings, all the ways in which
I have displeased You. Help me now to let go of
anything that is not of You, anything of darkness,
anything of sin, anything that is offensive to You,
anything that could keep me from uniting myself
with You. I especially repent of _____
(*any specific sins that come to mind*).

Mary, come in with your broom and sweep
my heart clean of all distractions and impurities
so that I may more worthily enter the heart of
Jesus with you.

—Vinny Flynn

BEFORE EACH READING

*Through the readings, God speaks to us, opening up "the
mystery of redemption and salvation and offering spiritual nourishment; . . . Christ himself is present through
his word in the midst of the faithful."*

—*The General Instruction of the Roman Missal, no. 55*

L ORD, help me to realize that You are speaking directly to me through these readings.
Help me to listen closely to Your Word; and, like
Mary, let me ponder it in my heart and respond
fully to it in my life.

THE RESPONSORIAL PSALM

The responsorial psalm is not just something to be recited but "is an integral part of the Liturgy of the Word" and has "great liturgical and pastoral importance, since it fosters meditation on the Word of God."

—*The General Instruction of the Roman Missal, no. 61*

L ORD, help me to pray this psalm with my whole mind and heart, reflecting on the beauty and truth of Your Word and responding faithfully to Your call for me to hear and fulfill Your will.

BEFORE THE GOSPEL

Priest or deacon: "A reading from the holy Gospel according to . . ."

Response: "Glory to You, O Lord."

Then, as you make the sign of the cross on your forehead, lips, and heart, pray silently:

"May the Word of God be in my mind, on my lips, and in my heart."

BEFORE THE CREED

"The purpose of the Creed . . . is that the whole gathered people may respond to the Word of God proclaimed in the readings . . . and that they may also honor and confess the great mysteries of the faith."

—*The General Instruction of the Roman Missal, no. 67*

LORD, fill me with Your grace so that I may recite the Creed with deep faith and conviction, to honor and proclaim these wondrous mysteries.

BEFORE THE PRAYER
OF THE FAITHFUL

In the Prayer of the Faithful, "the people respond . . . to the Word of God which they have received in faith and . . . offer prayers to God for the salvation of all."

—The General Instruction of the Roman Missal, no. 69

JESUS, help me not to be distracted as I join in offering these intercessions. Help me to really focus on each intention and offer it to You.

———— ✦ ————

"Naked I hung on the Cross
with arms outstretched,
offering Myself freely
to God the Father
for your sins
(Isa 53:7; Heb 9:28) . . .

You, too, must willingly
offer yourself daily
to Me in the Eucharist."

—Thomas a Kempis[5]

THE LITURGY OF THE EUCHARIST

"I appeal to you therefore, brothers
and sisters . . . to present your bodies
as a living sacrifice, holy and
acceptable to God."

—Rom 12:1 NRSVCE

THE PREPARATION OF THE GIFTS

The Offertory is not just a time to have a collection or sing a hymn while we wait for the "important" part of the Mass. It is a time to unite our personal offering to the eternal offering of Christ to the Father and to make the intention of His offering our own—atonement for our sins and the sins of the whole world.

Upon This Paten

HEAVENLY Father, I place myself upon this paten with my whole being, my soul, my body, with my intellect and my will; for I offer You all that I am and have.

I place upon this paten, all my joys, my sorrows of today, my work with its fatigue, my crosses with their bitterness.

I place also upon this paten all those whom I love, those who do me good, those who have done me good, those who have recommended themselves to my prayers. I unite all this to the offering of Jesus for the salvation of souls.[6]

Into the Chalice

WITH this drop of water that represents me, I cast into the chalice with Jesus every moment of my life so that all may be sanctified, super-naturalized in the blood of Christ, and pass through Him to the Adorable Trinity.

I cast also into the chalice and I offer You the life and sufferings of those who do not offer them, that their lives and sufferings may be united to those of Christ, who suffered as they do and who died for them.[7]

Eternal and Almighty Father

ETERNAL and Almighty Father, through the Immaculate Heart of Mary and the ministry of the priest, I offer You Jesus, Your beloved Son, and I offer myself through Him, with Him, and in Him, for His intentions, on behalf of all creatures and all creation, for Your greatest glory.

THE WASHING OF HANDS

As he washes his hands, the priest says a silent prayer, which you can pray in your heart, as both a prayer for him and for yourself:

"Wash me, O Lord, from my iniquity and cleanse me from my sins."

THE PREFACE

At the beginning of each Preface, the priest prays that the Lord may be with us and invites us to lift up our hearts and give thanks. Since, in our final response, we proclaim that "it is right and just" to give Him thanks, it's appropriate to take a moment and actually thank Him in some way:

YES, Lord, I lift my heart up to You. Thank You for all the ways You have blessed me.

THE SANCTUS

At the end of the Preface, we are encouraged to join the angels in their unending hymn of praise. As you recite or sing the Sanctus, take a moment to recognize and acknowledge this gift of participation in the heavenly liturgy.

LORD, God, help me not to miss this moment when heaven and earth come together to praise You. Help me to realize that this is not our "Holy, Holy, Holy"—that we're not singing our own little song of praise—but that *we're actually joining* the hymn that the angels are singing all the time. Thank You, Lord!

—Vinny Flynn

"I see the angelic choirs giving
You honor without cease and all
the heavenly powers praising You
without cease, and without cease
they are saying, 'Holy, Holy, Holy!'"

—St. Faustina, *Diary*, 80

THE ELEVATION OF THE HOST

As we gaze on the Lord with the eyes of faith during each of the elevations, we would do well to acknowledge His presence with a brief prayer of praise and adoration, such as the ones given here or any other words that come to mind.

"My Lord and my God!"

—St. Thomas (Jn 20:28)

O Sacrament Most Holy, O Sacrament Divine, all praise and all thanksgiving be every moment Thine.

O Sacred Flesh, pierced for love of me, transform me into love.

THE ELEVATION OF THE CHALICE

"O Blood and Water, which gushed forth from the Heart of Jesus, as a fount of mercy for us, I trust in You!"

—St. Faustina, Diary, 84

The above prayer has become known as The Conversion Prayer. Jesus promised St. Faustina that when she prayed this prayer with faith and a contrite heart on behalf of a sinner, He would give that soul the grace of conversion (see Diary, 186–187).

Lord, let Your Precious Blood wash me clean, deliver me from all that is not of You, and heal all that blocks me from receiving Your Love.

O Lord, I believe. Help my unbelief.

—Based on Mk 9:24

My God, I believe, I adore, I hope, and I love You. I ask pardon for those who do not believe, do not adore, do not hope, and do not love You.

—Prayer of the Angel, Fatima, 1916

THE SIGN OF PEACE

After offering a sign of peace to those around you, you can ask the Lord to also bless those you love with peace.

LORD Jesus, don't let this blessing of peace stop here with us, but let it extend also to _____ [*any of your loved ones who come to mind*] and to all those who are most in need of Your peace.

THE BREAKING OF THE BREAD

After the sign of peace, you can silently join the priest as he breaks the Host over the paten, places a small piece in the chalice, and prays quietly:

"May this mingling of the Body and Blood of our Lord Jesus Christ bring eternal life to us who receive it."

And you can add:

GOD, help me not to focus on myself, but let me, like Jesus, become bread broken for others.

THE PRIEST'S PRAYER
OF PREPARATION

After the Lamb of God, you can silently join the priest as he quietly prays in preparation for his reception of Communion.

LORD Jesus Christ, Son of the living God, who, by the will of the Father and the work of the Holy Spirit, through Your death gave life to the world, free me by this, Your most holy Body and Blood, from all my sins and from every evil; keep me always faithful to Your commandments and never let me be parted from You.

—From the Order of Mass in the Roman Missal

Or:

MAY the receiving of Your Body and Blood, Lord Jesus Christ, not bring me to judgment and condemnation but, through Your loving mercy, be for me protection in mind and body, and a healing remedy.

—From the Order of Mass in the Roman Missal

AS THE PRIEST RECEIVES

This is a perfect time to offer a prayer for the priest. You can say the prayer below or any other prayer that comes to mind, or you can simply let your heart surge to God for him.

LORD, thank You for the gift of this priest, who makes it possible for me to enter into communion with You. Bless him, Lord, strengthen him, and fill him to overflowing with Your love.

"Receiving Communion means
entering into communion
with Jesus Christ. . . .

What is given us here
is not a piece of a body,
not a thing, but him,
the Resurrected one himself—
the person who shares himself
with us in love. . . .

This means
that receiving Communion
is always a personal act."

—Joseph Cardinal Ratzinger[8]

COMMUNION PRAYERS

"If the angels could be jealous of men,
they would be so for one reason:
Holy Communion."

—St. Maximilian Kolbe

PREPARING FOR THE
COMING OF THE KING

WHAT am I, and who are You, O Lord, King of eternal glory? O my heart, are you aware of who is coming to you today? Yes, I know, but—strangely—I am not able to grasp it. Oh, if He were just a king, but He is the King of kings, the Lord of lords. Before Him, all power and domination tremble. He is coming to my heart today. . . . I hear Him approaching. I go out to meet Him and invite Him.

—St. Faustina, *Diary*, 1810

A Living Tabernacle

MARY, Mother of the Lord,
show us what it means
to enter into communion with Christ.
You offered your own flesh,
your own blood to Jesus
and became a living tabernacle,
allowing yourself to be penetrated
in body and spirit by His presence.
I ask you, Holy Mother,
to help me to offer myself
to Jesus with you
and to allow myself
to be penetrated by that same presence,
so that I may follow Him faithfully,
day after day, along whatever paths
He leads me.

—Vinny Flynn[9]

"If the Church and the Eucharist
are inseparably united, the same can
be said of Mary and the Eucharist."

—Pope St. John Paul II
The Church of the Eucharist, no. 57

To Your Loving Heart

HOW great, O my Jesus, is the extent of Your excessive love! You have prepared for me, of Your most precious Body and Blood, a divine banquet, where You give me Yourself without reserve. What has urged You to such an outpouring of mercy? Nothing but Your own most loving Heart.

—St. Gertrude[10]

Holy Spirit, Be My Guide

HOLY Spirit, be my Guide and Helper in this most sacred hour, as I prepare myself to receive the Most Holy Sacrament. Only through confidence in You, my God and Sanctifier, who are infinite Love itself, do I, a poor sinner, dare to approach Your altar. Enlighten my understanding, purify my heart, direct my will, strengthen my faith, enliven my hope, inflame my desire, enkindle my love, that I may receive the Gift of heaven worthily.[11]

To the Wounded Healer

LORD, Jesus, Wounded Healer, heal me from all the wounds of my past life and purify my heart, that I may become a fitting dwelling for the awesome splendor and consuming fire of Your Majesty.

—Vinny Flynn

Suscipe

TAKE, O Lord, and receive all my liberty, my memory, my understanding, and my entire will, all that I have and possess. You have given it to me; to You, Lord, I return it. All is Yours; dispose of it wholly according to Your will. Give me only Your love and Your grace; that's enough for me.

—St. Ignatius of Loyola

Prayer of St. Angela

THIS Sacrament really contains You, O my God, You whom the Angels adore, in whose presence the Spirits and mighty Powers tremble. Oh, if we could only see You clearly as they do, with what reverence would we approach this Sacrament, with what humility would we receive You!

—St. Angela of Foligno

DIVINE UNION

SENSES cannot tell me You are here,
In my heart the fragrance of Your love.
O Present and emptying One,
Awaken my hunger for the fullness of You.

Hidden and transforming God of longing,
My very self the substance You desire,
Each person the enclosure
Of Divine union here,

And nearer to us, You could not come.
Nearer to us, You could not come.

—Erin Flynn

FAITH

ETERNAL God, who can understand the depths of Your wisdom, the measure of Your power, and the greatness of Your love? I believe that You, the Son of God, are the living Bread from heaven. I believe that You are present, really and truly, Body and Soul, Divinity and Humanity, in the Holy Sacrament of the Altar. I believe that Your Body is really food and Your Blood is really drink. I believe that today I shall really partake of Your Holy Table. All this I believe because You have revealed it. Strengthen my faith, dear Jesus![12]

HUMILITY

JESUS, who am I that You should work such wonders for my sake? How dare I, a poor sinner, approach You, my God and Savior, the source of infinite purity and sanctity? St. John, pure and holy, considered himself unworthy to loose the straps of Your sandals. The angels conceal their faces out of reverence for You, but I am to receive You into my soul.

My extreme need of You must be my excuse. I rely upon Your mercy and goodness; I cast myself upon Your love. Help me, my Jesus, and fill up the emptiness of my heart. Take out of it every sinful affection. Wash my soul from sin by the grace of this Holy Communion, and graciously remove everything that might hinder Your grace from changing me from the poor sinner that I am into a saint.

Lord, I am not worthy that You should come to me. I would not dare approach Your Holy Table if You had not commanded me. Obedient to Your wish and command, because I love You and desire my salvation, I approach, feeling keenly my unworthiness and confessing: Lord, I am not worthy that You should come to me.[13]

CONTRITION

JESUS, I am a poor weak creature. How often has sin stained my soul! I am easily inclined to evil; I am inconstant in doing good. How many graces You have given me; how many times I have been unfaithful to You! I am truly sorry, O God of my heart, not only for not having loved You in the past, but for having rejected Your grace and friendship, turned my back on You, and offended You. Merciful Lord, I grieve with all my heart for this ingratitude. I sincerely detest all the sins that I have committed, because by them I have offended You, infinite Goodness. I trust that You have already forgiven me. Let me not hurt You again. Wash my soul in Your most precious Blood.[14]

"It is not so much we who receive Christ as Christ who receives us, incorporating us into Himself."

—Bishop Fulton Sheen, *This Is the Mass*

Prayer of St. Thomas Aquinas Before Communion

ALMIGHTY eternal God, behold, I come to the Sacrament of Your Only Begotten Son, our Lord Jesus Christ, as one sick to the physician of life, as one unclean to the fountain of mercy, as one blind to the light of eternal brightness, as one poor and needy to the Lord of heaven and earth.

I ask, therefore, for the abundance of Your immense generosity, that You may graciously heal my infirmity, wash away my defilement, give light to my blindness, enrich my poverty, clothe my nakedness, so that I may receive the bread of Angels, the King of kings and Lord of lords, with such reverence and humility, such contrition and devotion, such purity and faith, such purpose and intention as are conducive to the salvation of my soul.

Grant, I pray, that I may receive not only the Sacrament of the Lord's Body and Blood, but also its full grace and power.

Oh most gentle God, grant that I may so receive the Body of Your Only Begotten Son our Lord Jesus Christ, which He took from the Virgin Mary, that I may merit to be incorporated into His Mystical Body and counted among its members.

Oh most loving Father, grant that I may at last gaze for ever upon the unveiled face of Your beloved Son, whom I, a wayfarer, propose to receive now under the veil of this Sacrament.

Bread of My Soul

I ADORE You, my Saviour, present here as God and man, in soul and body, in true flesh and blood. I acknowledge and confess that I kneel before Your Sacred Humanity, which was conceived in Mary's womb, and lay in Mary's bosom; which grew up to man's estate, and by the Sea of Galilee called the twelve, wrought miracles, and spoke words of wisdom and peace; which in due season hung on the cross, lay in the tomb, rose from the dead, and now reigns in heaven.

I praise, and bless, and give myself wholly to You who are the true Bread of my soul, and my everlasting joy.

—Adapted from a prayer by
John Henry Cardinal Newman

WATER AND WINE

OH Lord, You were not tainted by the unclean woman who touched the hem of Your garment and was healed. Your holiness was not diminished by sitting with sinners or allowing a penitent heart to wash Your feet with her tears. You draw Your wounded people to You—raising our fallen humanity as the water mingles with the wine—that we might be healed, and that we might be one with You.

I come now as one in a crowd but aware that You see me as if I were really the only one. I am a sinner, Lord, but Your mercy is greater than my sin, and Your love gives me the courage to come in my brokenness. I walk forward wanting not only to touch You, but to receive You into my body. I don't understand how You, the One who cannot be contained, are going to enter and become part of me, but I know that this is exactly what You desire.

Come then, Lord, and with Your whole being, concealed in this heavenly food I now consume, enter the chamber of my solitude and consume me. Don't let my weaknesses or my doubt hinder the power of Your Presence. I repent, Lord, and I choose to will what You will. Let this Holy Communion change me.

Let me leave here different because You are within. Move inside me until there is no darkness to keep me from seeing as You see. Eradicate the fear, the self-love, and everything that takes me away from You, until there is only light, until I trust You completely, until I love like You.

—Erin Flynn

FORGIVE ME, LORD

O LORD and Master, Jesus Christ, my God: You alone have power to absolve us from sins. Forgive all my transgressions, committed deliberately or through human frailty, in word or by deed. Grant that, without condemnation, I may partake of Your divine, glorious, most pure, and life-giving Mysteries. Let my sharing in Your Body and Blood be for the forgiveness of my sins and for the healing of my soul and body, as well as for a pledge of the life to come in Your kingdom; for You are a merciful and gracious God; and we glorify You, Father, Son, and Holy Spirit, now and always and forever.

—St. John Damascene

SANCTIFY MY SOUL AND BODY

O LORD my God, how well I know that I am unworthy that You should enter into the temple of my soul. But I pray that, as You humbled Yourself and became man for our sake, You now also be patient with my lowliness. As You did not refuse to enter the house of Simon and dine there with sinners, now enter the abode of my humble and sinful soul. As You did not reject the sinful woman who approached and touched You, in like manner, do not reject me, a sinner, as I come to You and also touch You. Grant that I partake of Your most pure Body and precious Blood for the health of my soul and body, for the remission of my sins, for my protection against attacks of the Devil, for the increase of Your divine grace, and for the inheritance of Your heavenly kingdom. O gracious Lord, sanctify my soul and body, and make me worthy to stand at Your right hand with all Your saints.

—St. John Chrysostom

SO GREAT A GIFT

OH my God, holiness is fitting for Your House, and yet You make Your home within me. My Lord, my Savior, You come to me hidden under the appearance of earthly things, yet in that very flesh and blood, which You took from Mary. My God, You see me as I cannot even see myself. . . . When I say to You, "Lord, I am not worthy," You alone understand in their fullness the words I use. You alone see how unworthy so great a sinner is to receive the One Holy God, whom the Seraphim adore with trembling. You see all the stains and scars of my past sins, all my bad habits, all my disordered desires, all my wayward thoughts, all my weakness and misery. And yet You come!

O Lord, Help me to be more worthy of so great a gift. Give me a true perception of things unseen, and make me truly, practically, and in the details of life, prefer You to anything on earth, and the future world to the present.

—Adapted from a prayer by
John Henry Cardinal Newman

Grant That I May Receive You

LORD, grant that I may receive You with the purity, humility, and love with which Your most holy Mother received You, and with the fervor and spirit of the saints.[15]

O Come Abide in Me

JESUS, You come to me,
You, Word made flesh for me,
You, Lord, Who died for me,
You, Love made Food for me.
O come, abide in me!

Come, Jesus, even to me,
To one redeemed by You,
To one in love with You,
To one who longs for You.
O come, abide in me!

My Jesus, come to me
To reign upon Your throne,
To reign supreme alone,
To make me all Your own.
O come, abide in me![16]

"I am the food of full-grown men. Grow and you shall feed on me. But you shall not change me into your own substance, as you do with the food of your body. Instead, you shall be changed into me."

—St. Augustine, *Confessions*

A True Temple

LORD Jesus, as I eat Your Body and drink Your Blood, may Your charity pour into my soul, till at length love of others so springs up in my heart that no wicked hatred, nor deep envy, nor strong malice can remain in it.

For the sake of Your holy Body, pardon the faults I have committed through the frailty of my flesh. O Christ, who alone are all pure, by the power of Your grace wash away every spot from my mind, and every stain from my soul.

Oh God, who are the true peace, keep my soul undisturbed, and my mind at rest in You; for where there is peace, You Yourself are present, and where You are, all that is there is Yours. Come therefore, O Lord, take possession of me forever, and let me be a true temple of Your Holy Spirit.[17]

JUST BEFORE YOU RECEIVE

Trusting, I Come to You

OH Lord, I know that I am unworthy to receive Your Holy Body and Precious Blood, and that if I do not first discern the Body and Blood of Christ my God, I eat and drink condemnation to myself. But trusting in Your loving kindness, I come to You who have said: "He that eats my Body and drinks my Blood shall dwell in me and I in him."

Therefore, O Lord, treat me, Your sinful servant, according to Your great mercy, and grant that these Holy Gifts may be for me healing, purification, enlightenment, protection, salvation, the sanctification of my soul and body, and that they may expel every disordered imagination, sinful deed, or work of the evil one. May they move me to rely completely on You; to love You always; to firmly amend my life and stay true to this intention; and may they effect in me the increase of virtue, the continual indwelling of the Holy Spirit, and the defense against anything that would keep me from eternal life with You.

—St. Basil

Prepare My Heart

MARY, you were the first one asked to believe that God himself wanted to take flesh in you.

Come now into my heart, and help me to believe that this same God wants to live in me. Prepare my heart to receive Him, sweeping it clean of anything impure or unholy. And as I say "Amen," let it be a "*Fiat*," a complete "yes" to His will and a joyful acceptance of His life within me.

—Vinny Flynn

"Let everyone be struck with fear,
the whole world tremble,
and the heavens exult when Christ,
the Son of the living God,
is present on the altar in the hands of a priest!
O wonderful loftiness and stupendous dignity!
O sublime humility! O humble sublimity!
The Lord of the universe, God and the Son of God,
so humbles Himself that He hides Himself
for our salvation
under an ordinary piece of bread!"

—St. Francis

AS YOU RECEIVE

Fiat/Amen (Short Form)

YES, Lord, Amen. *Fiat*. Let it be done to me according to Your word. Yes, Lord, take flesh in me. Let me become living Eucharist, reflecting Your love to all I meet.

Fiat/Amen (Long Form)

AMEN! Yes, Lord, I believe that You are truly present here, Body and Blood, Soul and Divinity, hidden under what still looks like bread. Yes, Lord, I believe that You actually want to live in me, flesh of my flesh.

Fiat, Lord! Let it be done to me according to Your will. Live in me. Let Your whole "mode of being" pass into me—Your thoughts, Your feelings, Your attitudes, Your values, Your way of seeing and living and loving.

Keep me conscious of Your presence within me as I leave this church, and let me bring You with me into the world. Let me become living Eucharist, a living tabernacle of Your love.

Let me be, like Mary, a living monstrance, bringing Your love and the power of Your Spirit to all I meet, so that they, like the babe in Elizabeth's womb, may leap for joy at the tenderness of Your touch.

—Vinny Flynn[18]

My Communion Prayers

My Communion Prayers

My Communion Prayers

I Am He

Where are you going?
You, my beloved,
Sit with me in the stillness,
Breathe deeply of my love.

I am He who guides your days
and guards your nights,
I am He who calms your fears,
I am He who gives you strength
when you are weary,
I am He, I am He.

Do you rush to the busyness of your day?
Wait awhile,
It will all be there still,
My love will prepare you.

I am He who surrounds you with beauty,
I am He who holds you when you're hurting,
I am He who loves you
when all else fades away,
I am He, I am He,
Breathe deeply of my love.

—Erin Flynn

THANKSGIVING PRAYERS

*"The minutes that follow Communion
are the most precious we have in our lives."*
—St. Mary Magdalene di Pazzi

Transform Me into Yourself

HOW fortunate I am, Lord! I have just received You as the Food of my soul. When I partake of food, I change it into my own body; but when You give Yourself to me as food, You wish to transform me into Yourself. I earnestly beg of You to do so through this Holy Communion.[19]

For Purity of Heart

WHAT has passed our lips as food, O Lord, may we possess in purity of heart, that what has been given to us in time, may be our healing for eternity.

—From the Order of Mass in the *Roman Missal*

GRATITUDE

IN gratitude I draw close to You
Because You come to me in all my misery,
In all my weakness.
I am little, and You are the God of all.

Yet You are content to enter me,
Hiding all Your glory
Until You are concealed within,
Bursting forth then
To touch every place
That I release to You.

In gratitude I draw close to You
Because I want only to sit with You now,
Not asking, not speaking of my love,
Of my problems,
Or even of Your greatness.
Not talking at all, but just
Being. Here. With You
Dwelling inside me.

—Erin Flynn

AN ACT OF THANKSGIVING

WHO am I, O God of infinite goodness, that You permit me to partake of this bread of angels? How am I the object of such unspeakable mercy?

Come, all you angels and saints of God, and I will recount to you what great things our Lord has done for my soul. He has raised me out of the dust, and delivered me from the bonds of sin; He has told me not to be dejected, because He Himself will be my support and my strength; and though I have forsaken Him by my repeated falls, yet behold He calls me once more, and invites me to receive the bread of life, that, as He made me, so I may ever live by Him.

What thanks can I give You, O merciful Jesus, Savior of the world? What return shall I make to You for all You have done for my soul? Were I to give all I have in acknowledgment of Your love, it would still be as nothing; for You, Lord, have poured forth Yourself upon me, and given me even all that You are. And if, in thanksgiving for Your mercies, I were to lay before You my body and soul, my life, liberty, and all I possess, what would they be, when compared to the blessings You have here bestowed on me?

What can I give You that could be equal to what I receive, O Infinite One? You have mercifully given Yourself to me for the food of my soul; and now behold I simply offer You all that I have, all that I am, all that I possess. To You I make a full surrender of them all, that, being wholly Yours, I may now no longer cling to my own will, but may live for You alone.[20]

Prayer of St. Thomas Aquinas After Communion

I GIVE You thanks, O Eternal Father, for having, out of Your pure mercy, without my deserving it, been pleased to feed my soul with the body and blood of Your only son, and I beg You that this Holy Communion may not be to my condemnation, but be instead for the effectual remission of all my sins.

May it strengthen my faith, encourage me in the practice of good works, deliver me from my sinful habits, remove from me all concupiscence, perfect me in charity, patience, humility, obedience, and all other virtues.

May it be a firm defense against all the snares of my enemies, visible and invisible; prudently moderate my inclinations, both carnal and spiritual; closely unite me to You, the only true God; and finally settle me in unchangeable bliss, by admitting me, though an unworthy sinner, to be a guest at Your divine banquet, where You, with the Son and the Holy Spirit, are the true light, eternal fullness, everlasting joy, and perfect happiness of all the saints!

Gracious and Holy God

GRACIOUS and Holy God, please give me: intellect to understand You, reason to discern You, diligence to seek You, wisdom to find You, a spirit to know You, a heart to meditate upon You, ears to hear You, eyes to see You, a tongue to proclaim You, a way of life pleasing to You, patience to wait for You, and perseverance to look for You. Grant me a perfect end—Your holy presence, a blessed resurrection, and life everlasting.

—St. Benedict of Nursia

"Let us detain ourselves
lovingly with Jesus."

—St. Teresa of Jesus

STAY WITH ME, LORD

STAY with me, Lord, for it is necessary to have You present so that I do not forget You. You know how easily I abandon You.

Stay with me, Lord, because I am weak, and I need Your strength, that I may not fall so often.

Stay with me, Lord, for You are my life, and without You I am without fervor.

Stay with me, Lord, for You are my light, and without You I am in darkness.

Stay with me, Lord, to show me Your will.

Stay with me, Lord, so that I may hear Your voice and follow You.

Stay with me, Lord, for I desire to love You very much and always be in Your company.

Stay with me, Lord, and help me be faithful to You.

Stay with me, Lord, and let my poor soul be a place of consolation for You, a nest of Love.

Stay with me, Lord, for it is You alone I look for, Your Love, Your Grace, Your Will, Your Heart, Your Spirit; because I love You and ask no other reward but to love You more and more. Amen.

—Adapted from Padre Pio's
Prayer After Holy Communion

Anima Christi

Soul of Christ, sanctify me.
Body of Christ, save me.
Blood of Christ, inebriate me.
Water from the side of Christ, wash me.
Passion of Christ, strengthen me.
Oh good Jesus, hear me.
Within Your wounds, hide me.
Separated from You let me never be.
From the evil one, protect me.
At the hour of my death, call me,
And close to You bid me,
That with Your saints I may praise You
Forever and ever. Amen.

—Traditionally attributed to St. Thomas Aquinas

Draw Me to You

Oh draw me now entirely to You, divine Lover;
my mind with all its thoughts, my heart with
all its desires and affections, my will with all its
actions, my body with all its senses, that I may live
no longer in myself, Jesus, but in You!

—St. Peter Julian Eymard

Act of Love

O MY God, what return can I make for this tremendous gift, or what shall I do to acknowledge it as much as it deserves? Is it possible I should not continually love You, after such manifest proofs of Your love? You have loved me to such an excess as to lay down Your life for my sake; and shall I not make so small a return to such boundless love, as to live only for You? You have communicated Yourself at present entirely to me; and shall I not from this moment remain wholly Yours?

Permit me not, O God, to be ungrateful, or inattentive to Your love and my own salvation: I declare, therefore, in Your presence, that I will in the future be faithful to You, and never depart from You by the least disobedience. I will never forget Your goodness and mercy to me. I will love You with my whole heart; for You, O Lord, are my strength, my support, my refuge, and deliverer—You are my God and my all. What is there in heaven or on earth I should love in preference to You, the God of my heart, the inheritance and only happiness for which I strive? You I have chosen, and nothing shall prevail on me to change.

An Oblation

WHAT pledge can I give, O my Savior, to show You how sincere is the love I have professed to You? I have nothing worthy of You, and if I had, I have nothing but what is Yours; but such is Your goodness, that You are content to accept from us what is already Your own.

So then, behold, I here offer to You my body and soul, which are both now sanctified by Your divine presence; I consecrate them to You forever, since You have chosen them for Your temple; my body to be continually employed in Your service, and never more to become an instrument of sin; my soul to know You, to love You, and be evermore faithful to You.

Bless, O Lord, the offering which I here make You. "Bless, O Lord, this house." Do not permit my body to be defiled by sensual pleasure, nor my soul by a will to commit any grave sin; for, as I am now resolved to serve You with body and soul, I will labor to correct any evil inclinations. I renounce all my worldly desires, my sinful inclinations, my anger, my pride, my self-love, my own will, and whatever else would offend You.

I Give You My Whole Being

O JESUS, continue to grant me Your divine life. Let Your pure and noble Blood throb with all its might in my heart. I give You my whole being. Transform me into Yourself and make me capable of doing Your holy will in all things and of returning Your love. . . . May Your pure and omnipotent love be the driving force of all my actions.

—St. Faustina, *Diary*, 832

To Yield My Will

DEAREST Jesus, . . . through this Holy Communion, which I have just received, let me abide in You. . . . Help me to abide in Your love by doing Your Will perfectly and by preferring Your desires to my own. I am determined to make Your interests my own and to yield myself to You entirely, without counting the cost, reserving nothing and taking nothing back.

I rely with absolute confidence upon Your wisdom, Your power, Your strength, and Your love. . . . Grant that my soul may remain given up to You . . . and that Your action may become so powerful that my soul may be carried on to ever greater holiness. . . .

My beloved Savior, may Your coming to me establish between Your thoughts and mine, between Your sentiments and mine, between Your Will and my will, such an exchange, such a oneness, that I may have no other thoughts, no other sentiments, no other desires than those of Your Sacred Heart—and all this through love. May love yield my will to You, and through it, all my being, all my energies, and all that I am.[21]

I Give Myself to You

LORD Jesus, as You have given Yourself to me, now let me give myself to You. I give You my body that it may be chaste and pure. I give You my soul that it may be free from sin. I give You my heart that it may always love You. I give You every breath that I shall breathe, especially my last. I give You myself in life and in death, that I may be Yours forever and ever.

No Trace of Sin

MAY Your Body, O Lord, which I have eaten, and Your Blood which I have drunk, cleave to my very soul, and grant that no trace of sin be found in me, whom these pure and holy mysteries have renewed.

—From the Latin Rite of the Ablutions

Like a Crystal

I EXPOSE my heart to the action of Your grace like a crystal exposed to the rays of the sun. May Your image be reflected in it, O my God, to the extent that it is possible to be reflected in the heart of a creature. Let Your divinity radiate through me, O You who dwell in my soul.

—St. Faustina, *Diary*, 1336

This Divine Mystery

FATHER of mercy and God of all consolation, graciously look upon me and impart to me the blessing which flows from this holy Sacrament. Overshadow me with Your loving kindness, and let this divine Mystery bear fruit in me.

—St. Blase (*Radiating Christ*)

Abide in My Soul

JESUS, Son of God, at last You have come to abide in my soul. I welcome You with all my heart. I thank You for giving me the privilege of receiving You entirely, Your Divinity and Humanity, Your Body, Your Blood, Your Soul. May this Holy Communion produce all the effects in my soul which You intend it to produce. Let nothing stand in the way of Your grace.[22]

MY LIFE A RADIANCE OF YOURS

DEAR Jesus, help me to spread Your fragrance everywhere I go. Flood my soul with Your Spirit and life. Penetrate and possess my whole being so utterly that my life may only be a radiance of Yours.

Shine through me, and be so in me that every person I come in contact with may feel Your presence in my soul. Let them look up and see no longer me, but only You, Jesus!

Stay with me, and then I shall begin to shine as You shine, so that I may be a light to others. The light, Jesus, will be all from You; none of it will be mine. It will be You shining on others through me.

Let me thus praise You in the way You love best, by shining on those around me. Let me preach You without preaching, not by words but by example, by that catching force, the sympathetic influence of all I do, and in the evident fullness of the love my heart bears to You.

—John Henry Cardinal Newman

Mary, Give Me Your Heart

MARY, Mother of Jesus, give us your love, your heart, so beautiful, so pure, so immaculate, your heart so full of love and humility, that we may be able to love Jesus as you loved Him, and serve Him in the distressing disguise of the poor.

—Mother Teresa[23]

Late Have I Loved You

LATE have I loved You, O Beauty ever ancient, ever new, late have I loved You! You were within me, but I was outside, and it was there that I searched for You. In my unloveliness I plunged into the lovely things which You created. You were with me, but I was not with You. Created things kept me from You; yet if they had not been in You, they would not have been at all. You called, You shouted, and You broke through my deafness. You flashed, You shone, and You dispelled my blindness. You breathed Your fragrance on me; I drew in breath and now I pant for You. I tasted You; now I hunger and thirst for more. You touched me, and I burned for Your peace.

—St. Augustine

PETITION

I COME with a heart full of petitions,
A heart breaking with the heaviness
Of so much need.

But as I receive You, Jesus, I am silent.
I know it is good to ask,
That You love a generous and selfless soul.
But let my asking be but a motion now.
I move within and meet You,
Entering Your heart.
And with me come all those I care for,
All I have enclosed in my heart.

My love can only do them so much good,
But I nestle close
To feel the breathing of Your love,
The rhythmic beats of union
As my heart melts into Yours.

And they sit with me here
Resting—resting.

I bring them to bask in the Presence
Of the One who can meet
All their needs.

—Erin Flynn

Divine Master, Spouse of My Heart

DIVINE Master, Spouse of my heart, I will follow You everywhere with Mary, my Mother. Having You, do I not possess all riches? To love You and please You—is not that the greatest happiness of life? To share Your sacrifices, Your sufferings, Your death—is not that the most glorious victory of love? O my God, my mind is made up! I make no more conditions or reservations in my love for You. I will follow You in all things, yes, even to Calvary! Speak, pierce, cut, burn! My heart is altar and victim!

—St. Peter Julian Eymard

Our Lady of the Most Blessed Sacrament

OUR Lady of the Most Blessed Sacrament, pray for me that I may become, like your Son Jesus, Bread for the life of the world. Through Him, with Him and in Him, may my life be a joyful, living sacrifice of love and praise to the honor and glory of God our Father. Amen.

—Alice Claire Mansfield[24]

Prayer of Abandonment

FATHER, I abandon myself into Your hands; do with me what You will. Whatever You may do, I thank You: I am ready for all, I accept all. Let only Your will be done in me, and in all Your creatures. I wish no more than this, O Lord.

Into Your hands I commend my soul; I offer it to You with all the love of my heart, for I love You, Lord, and so need to give myself, to surrender myself into Your hands, without reserve, and with boundless confidence, for You are my Father.

—Blessed Charles de Foucauld

AT THE FINAL BLESSING

As the priest gives the final blessing and you make the sign of the cross, you can ask the Lord to extend that offering to others.

LORD, let this blessing extend also to _____ [*any of your loved ones or others who come to mind*] and to those who are in most need of it.

THE DISMISSAL

HELP ME TO UNDERSTAND

LORD, help me to understand fully that this is not just the end of the Mass, but a sending forth, whereby I am empowered to share with others what I have received.

AS I LEAVE THIS SACRED BANQUET

OH Lord, I have been to Your sacred banquet. I have been fed with the bread of angels, made the bread of mortal human beings. It is beyond me! Into my own being in the most intimate way You, the Savior of the world, have come to me. . . . O Lord, let me accept all that this day may bring as coming from You. As I leave this Sacred Banquet filled with the grace of this Holy Communion, may I bring You to others by kindness, by generosity, by forgiveness, by patience, by love. Help me to break out of the prison of my own self-concern, of what I think is important. Give me the grace to be You to others and to find You in them.

—Fr. Benedict Groeschel[25]

BEFORE LEAVING THE CHURCH

OVERFLOW

WHAT use is it if I receive You
and do not bear You to the world?
"Mary went in haste . . ."
What use is it
if I join myself to You in love
and do not love my brother?
"They'll know you are my disciples . . ."

Is it even possible to be
truly united to Goodness
and not share that goodness?
What kind of union is it,
if I stay my same self thereafter?

Do not allow me to remain as I am, Jesus.
Help me to prepare my heart
for true union with You,
a union that will reveal You to the world
uniquely through me.

For what use is it if You come to me
and I refuse You to my neighbor?
What use is it, Lord, if You fill me
and I do not overflow?

—Erin Flynn

A Host Lifted in Me

I CAME, with my sins, my troubles,
my weakness, my limitations.
I go with the life of Christ,
with the Host in my soul;
Let me go as a host,
offered with Him and for the love of Him
to all those I come
in contact with today.

Let me be to them a Christ,
loving with His love,
not with sentimentality and selfishness,
not asking for anything,
but with my own heart
an altar of sacrifice,
where He shall be offered for them,
in patience, in submission,
in compassion, in service,
in cooperation, in abnegation,
in sacrifice, in wrestling with self,
and, please God, in dying to self.
Let Him be a host lifted in me,
in places where otherwise
no Host comes.
Let me show His beauty,
His simplicity, His attractiveness,
in laughter, in tenderness,

in my interest in their affairs,
in seeing the good in them,
fostering their aspirations,
making myself, my heart—
not only the outside of me—
accessible to them.

Let me reveal Him even when I fail;
in humility, in acknowledging my faults
without servility, without morbidity,
without the vanity which is amazed
by its own failure;
but asking forgiveness and going on,
trusting Him.

Let me work with His devotion
to duty, to the will of God,
and for the glory of God.
Let my soul be His Nazareth.
Let Christ in me,
be among my fellow-workers,
and be in ways I shall not know,
light to them and strength.
Let them be happier because in me,
He has, with exquisite courtesy,
chosen to be among them.

I have been this morning in Heaven,
and Heaven has come to abide in me;
let me take Heaven with me into the world.[26]

Go With Me, Lord

AND now, Lord Jesus, I go from You for a while, but I hope not without You, who are my comfort and the ultimate fulfillment of my soul. To Your love and protection I entrust myself, this community, my relatives, my country, my friends, and my enemies. Love us, O Lord, change our hearts, and transform us into Yourself. May I be wholly employed in You and for You; and may Your love be the origin of all my thoughts, words, and deeds.

My Thanksgiving Prayers

My Thanksgiving Prayers

My Thanksgiving Prayers

"In this golden chalice I put
your sacramental communions.
In this silver chalice I put
your spiritual communions.
Both chalices
are quite pleasing to me."

—Our Lord to St. Catherine of Siena[27]

"The manner of receiving this
sacrament is twofold,
spiritual and sacramental.
The effect of a sacrament
can be secured if it is
received by desire.
Even by desiring it,
a person receives grace
whereby he is spiritually alive."

—St. Thomas Aquinas[28]

SPIRITUAL COMMUNION PRAYERS

"I love so much a soul's desire to receive Me
that I hasten to it each time
it summons Me by its yearnings."
—Jesus to St. Margaret Mary Alacoque[29]

AN ACT OF SPIRITUAL COMMUNION

MY Jesus, I believe that You are in the Blessed Sacrament. I love You above all things, and I long for You in my soul. Since I cannot now receive You Sacramentally, come at least spiritually into my heart. As though You have already come, I embrace You and unite myself entirely to You. Never permit me to be separated from You.

Visit Me With Your Grace

J ESUS, I turn toward the holy tabernacle where
You live hidden for love of me. I love You, O
my God. I cannot receive You in Holy Communion. Come, nevertheless, and visit me with Your
grace. Come spiritually into my heart. Purify it.
Sanctify it. Make it like Your own.

—Monsignor M. J. Doyle[30]

Mary, Place Him in My Soul

O IMMACULATE Queen of Heaven and
Earth, Mother of God and Mediatrix of
every grace: I believe that Your dearly beloved
Son, Our Lord Jesus Christ, is truly, really, and
substantially contained in the Most Blessed Sacrament. I love Him above all things, and I long to
receive Him into my heart.

Since I cannot now receive Him sacramentally, I ask You to place Him spiritually in my
soul. O my Jesus, I embrace You as One who
has already come, and I unite myself entirely to
You. Never permit me to be separated from You.
Amen.

I Long to be Filled

JESUS, as always my mind and heart are pulled in so many directions. In this moment, here, now, I remove myself from the noise, and enter the quiet of eternity. I unite myself to Your Eucharistic Presence, as You sit, loving us from all the tabernacles of the world.

Lord, I cannot receive You now in Holy Communion, but I long to be filled with You just the same. I open myself to You completely; to Your power, to Your wisdom, to Your love. Let everything I am be transformed by everything You are. I re-consecrate this day to You so that every thought, word, and deed will be filled with Your Presence.

—Erin Flynn

At the Foot of Your Altar

AS I cannot this day be present at the holy Mysteries, O my God, I transport myself in spirit to the foot of Your altar; I unite with the Church, which by the hands of the priest, offers to You, Father, Your beloved Son in the Holy Sacrifice; I offer myself with Him, by Him, and in His Name. I adore You, and thank You, imploring

Your mercy, invoking Your assistance, and praising You as my Creator.

Apply to my soul, O merciful Jesus, the grace You won for me on the Cross, made available in the present through the great gift of the Eucharist. Apply it also to those for whom I particularly wish to pray.

Though I cannot receive You physically in Holy Communion, I desire to receive You spiritually, that Your Blood may purify, Your Flesh strengthen, and Your Spirit sanctify me. May I never forget that You, my divine Redeemer, died for me; may I die in this world to all that is not of You, that hereafter I may live with You eternally. Amen.

MAY I EVER YEARN FOR YOU

LORD Jesus Christ, grant that my soul may hunger for You, the Bread of Angels, the Refreshment of holy souls, our daily and ever-satisfying Bread. May I ever yearn for You, seek You, find You, stretch towards You, reach You, meditate upon You, speak of You, and do all things for the praise and glory of Your holy name.

—From a prayer by St. Bonaventure

COME TO ME INCARNATE WORD

LORD, from where I am I come,
Entering Your Presence oh God of Love.
I cannot consume that heavenly food,
But come as if I've truly received You.

Come as though Your Presence fills me,
Come as though Your Blood runs through me,
Come and let our beings merge,
Come to me Incarnate Word.

Oh Jesus, bring me heaven's rest,
The Father's touch of tenderness,
The Spirit and all knees that bowed,
Bring to me the Eternal Now.

—Erin Flynn

"If you practice the holy exercise of
spiritual Communion several times
each day, within a month you will see
your heart completely changed."

—St. Leonard of Port Maurice

My Spiritual Communion Prayers

My Spiritual Communion Prayers

EUCHARISTIC
ADORATION

❖

"Communicating with Christ
demands that we gaze on him,
allow Him to gaze on us,
listen to him, get to know him.

Adoration is simply the
personal aspect of Communion. . . .

God is waiting for us
in Jesus Christ
in the Blessed Sacrament.
Let us not leave him
waiting in vain!

Let us not,
through distraction and lethargy,
pass by the greatest and
most important thing life offers us."

—Joseph Cardinal Ratzinger[31]

ADORATION PRAYERS

"Without adoration there is no transfiguration of the world."

—Joseph Cardinal Ratzinger[32]

Upon Entering the Chapel

ETERNAL Father, I offer You the Body and Blood, Soul and Divinity of Your dearly beloved Son, our Lord Jesus Christ, in atonement for our sins and those of the whole world. For the sake of His sorrowful Passion, have mercy on us and on the whole world.

—Prayer that Our Lord told St. Faustina to pray immediately upon entering the chapel (*Diary*, 476).

RADIATION PRAYER

LORD, here I am. Thank You for being here and for letting me be with You. Lord, You know all my limitations, all my weakness. You know how hard it is for me to keep my focus on You. You know how mixed my motives can be, how confused I get sometimes. But I am here, Lord, because I know I need You, and I want to be healed of everything that keeps me from being the person You created me to be.

So, I ask You, Lord, no matter what I'm able to do during this time—whether I pray or read, day-dream or sleep, or just sit here in a seemingly mindless way—bless me, Lord, and work on me. Cleanse me, change me, mold me, remake me in Your image.

I am here to Son-bathe, Lord, to expose myself to the healing rays of Your love and become more like You. Please let it be done, hour by hour by hour.

—Vinny Flynn

CONSECRATION TO THE
HEART OF JESUS

LORD Jesus, You invite me to come to You. So I come to Your Sacred Heart, the fountain of all mercy. I come with my sins, my misery, and my burdens. Cleanse me, transform me, and fill me with Your mercy.

Jesus, You invite me to take Your yoke. So I take up my daily cross, to walk in trust, in step with You. I offer You my whole self as a living sacrifice. Make me holy and acceptable to the Father, and make my heart like Yours. As Your Heart was pierced for me, pierce my heart to be a channel of mercy for others. Jesus, You invite me to learn from You. So teach me Your gentleness and humility. As a child dependent on Your mercy, I take refuge in Your Heart. I want to do Your will and glorify Your mercy.

Jesus, You promised to refresh me. So let me find peace by resting on Your Heart like John. I want to be present to You with my heart, and radiate Your presence to others.

—Fr. George Kosicki, CSB.
Based on Mt 11:28–30

CONSECRATION TO MARY
QUEEN OF THE EUCHARIST

MARY, wherever Jesus is, you are there with Him, so I know that you are present here now at His side, loving me as He loves me.

Here with you in His presence, like John at the foot of the cross, I receive you now as my Mother and consecrate myself to you once again. Mother of Mercy and my Mother, I offer myself completely to you. I place myself and all my loved ones under the mantle of your Immaculate Conception, trusting you to protect us from all sin, all harm, and all evil.

In your hands, Mary, I renew and ratify the vows of my baptism. I renounce Satan and all his works and resolve, with your help, to keep my gaze fixed on Jesus, following Him as you lead me, faithful to even the slightest inspirations of His Holy Spirit.

To you, I entrust all I am, all I have, and all I do—this present moment, my entire past, and all that is to come in the future. To you I surrender my dreams and desires, my plans and goals, my actions and decisions, my work with all its tasks and responsibilities, my health and recreation, my finances and material possessions, and even the value of any good that I do.

Mary, Queen of the Eucharist, I place my heart in your Immaculate Heart. Purify it and enthrone Jesus there, so that I may be, like you, a living tabernacle of His mercy, a living monstrance, radiating His love to all I meet.

—Vinny Flynn

"We ponder your steadfast love,
O God, in the midst of your temple."

—Ps 48:9 NRSVCE

TABERNACLE PRAYER

O PRISONER of Love, I lock up my poor heart in this tabernacle, that it may adore You without cease night and day. . . . On leaving the earth, O Lord, You wanted to stay with us, and so You left us Yourself in the Sacrament of the Altar, and You opened wide Your mercy to us. There is no misery that could exhaust You; You have called us all to this fountain of love, to this spring of God's compassion. Here is the tabernacle of Your mercy, here is the remedy for all our ills.

—St. Faustina, *Diary*, 80, 1747

To Penetrate the Veils

JESUS, on the altar I can see neither Your Humanity nor Your Divinity. For my senses, the sight, the taste, the touch, there are only the bread and wine. Give me the eye of faith to see through these appearances, to penetrate these veils and see You as You really are.[33]

The Angel's Prayer at Fatima

MOST Holy Trinity: Father, Son, and Holy Spirit, I adore You profoundly, and I offer You the most precious Body, Blood, Soul, and Divinity of Jesus Christ, present in all the tabernacles of the world, in reparation for the outrages, sacrileges, and indifference by which He is offended. Through the infinite merits of His most Sacred Heart and those of the Immaculate Heart of Mary, I beg of You the conversion of poor sinners.

"The human heart is converted by looking at Him whom our sins have pierced."

—*Catechism of the Catholic Church* 1432

O KING OF GLORY

O KING of Glory, though You hide Your beauty, yet the eye of my soul rends the veil. I see the angelic choirs giving You honor without cease, and all the heavenly Powers praising You without cease, and without cease they are saying: Holy, Holy, Holy.

—St. Faustina, *Diary*, 80

BY YOUR HOLY CROSS

I ADORE You, most Holy Lord Jesus Christ, present here and in all the tabernacles of the world; and I bless You; because by Your Holy Cross, You have redeemed the world.

—St. Francis of Assisi, adapted from the Raccolta, no. 74

PRAYER BEFORE A CRUCIFIX

M OST high, glorious God, cast Your light into the darkness of my heart. Give me right faith, firm hope, perfect charity, and profound humility, with wisdom and perception, O Lord, so that I may do what is truly Your holy will.

—St. Francis

Father God

FATHER God, You are indeed a Father
  "rich in mercy," slow to anger,
gracious and compassionate
to all who call upon You.

In praise and thanksgiving,
I offer this day to You.
In the name of Jesus,
and in union with Mary Immaculate,
St. Faustina, and all the saints and angels,
I ask for the grace
to become a living image of Your love,
a living monstrance of Your presence,
empowered by Your Holy Spirit
to call down Your blessing
upon all the people
and all the situations
I encounter today
as an instrument of Your mercy.

—Vinny Flynn

FATHER OF UNFAILING LIGHT

FATHER of unfailing light,
give that same light to me
as I call upon You.
May my lips praise You,
My life proclaim Your goodness,
my work give You honor,
and my voice celebrate You forever.

Loving Father,
may everything I do today
begin with Your inspiration
and continue with Your saving help.
May my work always find
its origin in You and,
through You, reach completion.

—Adapted from the Divine Office[34]

"If souls but understood the Treasure
they possess in the Divine Eucharist, . . .
the churches would overflow with adorers."

—Blessed Dina Belanger

Before You, Lord

To be here before You, Lord,
    that's all:
to shut the eyes of my body,
to shut the eyes of my soul,
and be still and silent,
to expose myself to You who are
here, exposed to me.

To be here before You,
the Eternal Presence,
I am willing to feel nothing, Lord,
to see nothing,
to hear nothing,
empty of all ideas, of all images,
in the darkness.

Here I am, simply,
to meet You without obstacles,
in the silence of faith,
before You, Lord.

But, Lord, I am not alone.
I am a crowd, Lord,
for people live within me.
I have met them,
they have come in,

they have settled down,
they have worried me,
they have tormented me,
they have devoured me,
and I have allowed it, Lord,
that they might be nourished and refreshed.

I bring them to You, too,
as I come before You.
I expose them to You
in exposing myself to You.

Here I am, here they are,
before You, Lord!

—Michel Quoist[35]

PRESENT TO THE ONE WHO IS PRESENT

MY God, I believe that You are truly present here under the appearance of bread. Help me to please You by being truly present to You, with my heart in the heart of Mary, trusting, rejoicing, and giving thanks.

—Fr. George Kosicki, CSB

To Mercy-Made-Flesh

LORD Jesus,
You are Mercy-Made-Flesh,
the visible "image
of the invisible God (Col 1:15)."
You are the Father's love
made present for us.

As I gaze upon You,
I see the Father,
"rich in mercy,"
raising His hand over me in blessing
and pouring into me,
through Your pierced Heart,
the very life of the Trinity
as a Fountain of Mercy.

Immersing myself
in this living stream
of blood and water,
flowing endlessly
from Your Heart,
I receive the Father's blessing
and recognize who I am
as a child of His love.

In You, Lord Jesus,
I see the reflection

of my own unique value
and dignity as a son/daughter
of the Father,
created in His image and likeness
and called to be holy as He is holy.

In You and with You,
I will forever call God my Father
And forever rejoice
in the awesome reality
that He loves me
even as He loves You (see Jn 17:23).

—Vinny Flynn

Prayer for Zeal

JESUS, You know how weak and sinful I am. I am often tempted, troubled, and discouraged. To You I come for remedy. I pray to You for comfort and help. You alone can help me. Inflame my coldness with the fire of Your love; enlighten my blindness with the brightness of Your presence; fill my poor soul with the treasures of Your grace. Enlighten my faith, strengthen my hope, and inflame my love, that all sinful inclinations may disappear in me, and that I may prefer death to ever again committing a single sin.[36]

Prayer to Our Lord Jesus Christ Crucified

BEHOLD, O good and loving Jesus, that I cast myself on my knees before You and, with the greatest fervor of spirit, I pray and beseech You to instill into my heart ardent sentiments of faith, hope and charity, with true repentance for my sins and a most firm purpose of amendment. With deep affection and sorrow I ponder intimately and contemplate in my mind Your five wounds, having before my eyes what the prophet David had already put in Your mouth about Yourself, O good Jesus: "They have pierced my hands and my feet; they have numbered all my bones" (Ps 21:17–18).

I Adore You, Lord and Creator

I ADORE You, Lord and Creator, hidden in the Blessed Sacrament. I adore You for all the works of Your hands, that reveal to me so much wisdom, goodness and mercy, O Lord. You have spread so much beauty over the earth, and it tells me about Your beauty, even though these beautiful things are but a faint reflection of You, Incomprehensible Beauty.

And although You have hidden Yourself and concealed Your beauty, my eye, enlightened by faith, reaches You, and my soul recognizes its Creator, its Highest Good; and my heart is completely immersed in prayer of adoration.

My Lord and Creator, Your goodness encourages me to converse with You. Your mercy abolishes the chasm, which separates the Creator from the creature. To converse with You, O Lord, is the delight of my heart. In You I find everything that my heart could desire. Here Your light illumines my mind, enabling it to know You more and more deeply. Here streams of graces flow down upon my heart. Here my soul draws eternal life.

O my Lord and Creator, You alone, beyond all these gifts, give Your own self to me and unite Yourself intimately with Your miserable creature. Here, without searching for words, our hearts understand each other. For this incomprehensible goodness of Yours, I adore You, O Lord and Creator, with all my heart and all my soul. And, although my worship is so little and poor, I am at peace because I know that You know it is sincere, however inadequate. . . .

—St. Faustina, *Diary*, 1692

Prayer of St. Gertrude

O SACRED Heart of Jesus, living and life-giving fountain of eternal life, infinite treasury of the Divinity, and glowing furnace of love, You are my refuge and my sanctuary. O loving and glorious Savior, consume my heart with that burning fire that ever inflames Your Heart.

Pour down on my soul those graces that flow from Your love. Let my heart be so united with Yours, that our wills may be one, and mine may in all things be conformed to Yours. May Your will be the rule of both my desires and my actions.

To the Sacred Heart

S ACRED Heart of Jesus, filled with infinite love, broken by my ingratitude, pierced by my sins, yet loving me still, accept the consecration that I make to You, of all that I am and all that I have. Take every faculty of my soul and body, and draw me, day by day, nearer and nearer to Your Sacred Side, and there, as I can bear the lesson, teach me Your blessed ways.

Ezekiel Prayer

COME now, Lord,
and sprinkle clean water upon me.
Cleanse me from all my impurities
and from all my idols.

Give me a new heart
and place a new spirit within me,
taking away my stony heart
and giving me a natural heart.

Put Your Spirit within me, Lord,
so that I may live by Your statutes,
and carefully observe Your decrees.

—Vinny Flynn, Adapted from Ez 36:25–27

Philippians Prayer

HELP me, Lord, to rejoice in You always, with no anxiety about anything. Help me in everything, by prayer and supplication with thanksgiving, to make my requests known to You.

—Adapted from Phil 4:4, 6

To Please You, Lord Jesus

MY Lord Jesus Christ, who, for the love You bear mankind, remain night and day in this Sacrament, full of tenderness and love, awaiting, calling, and welcoming all who come to visit You; I believe that You are present in the Sacrament of the Altar. I adore You from the depths of my nothingness, and I thank You for all the graces You have given me, especially for having given me Yourself in this Sacrament; for having given me Your most holy Mother Mary as my advocate, and for having called me to visit You in this church. . . .

My Jesus, I love You with my whole heart. I am sorry for having so often offended Your infinite goodness. I resolve, with Your grace, to displease You no more; and, unworthy as I am, I now consecrate myself completely to You. I entrust to You my will, my affections, my desires, and all that I possess. From now on, dispose of me and of all that I have entirely as You please. I ask for nothing but You and Your holy love, final perseverance, and the perfect fulfillment of Your will.

—St. Alphonsus Liguori

Teach Me, Mary

MARY, as I kneel here in the presence of your Son Jesus, I turn to you to help me adore Him more completely. Wherever Jesus is, you are with Him. It is thanks to your "fiat," your offering of your own body in sheer abandonment to God, that the Word became flesh in your womb. This was the first reception of Holy Communion, and when you gave birth to the Son of God, you were the first to adore His presence among us. Throughout your life you remained in communion with your Son, always united with Him in unselfish love. Teach me, Mary, how to adore Him as you do, how to remain always in His presence in complete union with His holy will.

—Vinny Flynn (based on Pope St. John Paul II)[37]

Jesus, My God, I Adore You

JESUS, my God, I adore You, here present in the Blessed Sacrament of the altar, where You wait day and night to be our comfort while we await Your unveiled presence in heaven. Jesus, my God, I adore You in all places where the Blessed Sacrament is reserved and where sins are committed against this Sacrament of Love. Jesus, my

God, I adore You for all time, past, present and future, for every soul that ever was, is, or shall be created.

Jesus, my God, who for us endured hunger and cold, labor and fatigue, I adore You. Jesus, my God, who for our sake deigned to subject Yourself to the humiliation of temptation, to the betrayal and defection of friends, to the scorn of Your enemies, I adore You. Jesus, my God, who for us endured the buffeting of Your passion, the scourging, the crowning with thorns, the heavy weight of the cross, I adore You. Jesus, my God, who, for my salvation and that of all mankind, were cruelly nailed to the cross and hung there for three long hours in bitter agony, I adore You. Jesus, my God, who for love of us did institute this Blessed Sacrament and offer Yourself daily for the sins of men, I adore You. Jesus, my God, who in Holy Communion became the food of my soul, I adore You. Jesus, for You I live. Jesus, for You I die. Jesus, I am Yours in life and death.

—Adapted from a prayer by
John J. Cardinal Carberry[38]

For a Moment I Am With You

OH Lord Jesus Christ, this day is very busy. I am distracted and pulled in many directions. There are concerns, worries, even fears. I am troubled about duties, failures, things to do that are beyond me. I come to Your presence from the din of life, the noise of the street, from the pleas and demands of others. And You are here. For a moment I am with You by the Sea of Galilee, on the Mount of Beatitudes, looking at the serene water and the green hills. You say, "Come to me, all you who are weary and find life burdensome, and I will refresh you." Your presence in the Eucharist reassures me that this is true.

—Fr. Benedict Groeschel, CFR[39]

Missionaries of Charity Prayer

DEAR Lord, the Great Healer, I kneel before You, since every perfect gift must come from You. I pray, give skill to my hands, clear vision to my mind, kindness and meekness to my heart. Give me singleness of purpose, strength to lift up a part of the burden of my suffering fellow men, and a true realization of the privilege that is mine. Take from my heart all guile and worldliness, that with the simple faith of a child, I may rely on You. Amen.[40]

To Be Like You, Lord

LORD Jesus, I place all my trust in You,
and I will follow You as Your disciple
every day of my life.
I repent of all my sins,
—even the tiniest sins—
all the ways I have turned away from You
or failed to reflect Your love to others.

I revoke any thoughts or words
that have been negative, judgmental,
or unkind,
and I replace them with blessing.
I forgive all who have ever hurt me
and I ask You to bless them with Your love.

Lord Jesus,
By the healing power
of Your Eucharistic presence,
restore me
in Your image and likeness
so that I may live
like You and with You forever.

—Vinny Flynn

The Petitions of St. Augustine

O LORD Jesus, let me know myself,
Let me know You,
And desire nothing else but only You.
Let me deny myself and love You,
And do all things for the sake of You.
Let me humble myself, and exalt You,
And think of nothing else but You.
Let me die to myself, and live in You,
And take whatever happens
As coming from You.
Let me forsake myself and walk after You,
And ever desire to follow You.
Let me flee from myself, and turn to You,
That so I may merit to be defended by You.
Let me fear for myself, let me fear You,
And be amongst those who are
Chosen by You.
Let me distrust myself, and trust in You,
And ever obey for the love of You.
Let me cleave to nothing but You,
And ever be poor for the sake of You.
Look upon me, that I may love You,
Call me, that I may see You,
And forever possess You.

THANK YOU FOR THIS HOUR

OH Lord, thank You for this hour of Eucharistic devotion. It comes as a time of peace, recollection, and healing. How privileged I am to spend an hour with You! It makes me feel like the apostles and the disciples who were able to speak quietly with You along the road, perhaps sitting under a tree in the evening.

What am I to say to You? You know everything about me. You know all my needs, all my failings and even my good intentions. In this hour I adore You as the infinite and Holy One of God. You and the Father are one, and You have promised that we will be one in You.

I give You thanks for all the blessings of my life, which I so seldom think of. I thank You for life itself, material and spiritual. I ask Your forgiveness and healing for all my short-comings and sins; all the times that unthinkingly I have failed You and fallen short of the grace that You gave me.

And finally I place before You confidently everyone that I care about, every concern that I have, every need of my life. I promise to trust You no matter what happens to me. You will bring good out of even the worst of it.

I do not ask You to change what is to be. Rather, in whatever there is to be, let me find Your will, Your holiness, and Your opportunity for me to grow. I will try to say, "I know that You are with me."

Finally, I redirect my life, my desires, my hopes, to You, not only for myself but for all whom I care about and for the whole world. May Your kingdom come. May Your Holy Spirit be with us. Send Him constantly to us as You promised You would at the Last Supper.

As I look at this mysterious sign, the white host, my eyes tell me nothing of who is there, but faith affirms in my heart that You, my Lord and God, are there. I thank You for this precious gift of faith.

—Fr. Benedict Groeschel, CFR[41]

FOR THE GRACE TO BE MERCIFUL TO OTHERS

I WANT to be completely transformed into Your mercy and to be Your living reflection, O Lord. May the greatest of all divine attributes, that of Your unfathomable mercy, pass through my heart and soul to my neighbor.

Help me, O Lord, that my eyes may be merciful, so that I may never suspect or judge from appearances, but look for what is beautiful in my neighbors' souls and come to their rescue.

Help me, that my ears may be merciful, so that I may give heed to my neighbors' needs and not be indifferent to their pains and moanings.

Help me, O Lord, that my tongue may be merciful, so that I should never speak negatively of my neighbor, but have a word of comfort and forgiveness for all.

Help me, O Lord, that my hands may be merciful and filled with good deeds, so that I may do only good to my neighbors and take upon myself the more difficult and toilsome tasks.

Help me, that my feet may be merciful, so that I may hurry to assist my neighbor, overcoming my own fatigue and weariness. My true rest is in the service of my neighbor.

Help me, O Lord, that my heart may be merciful so that I myself may feel all the sufferings of my neighbor. I will refuse my heart to no one. I will be sincere even with those who, I know, will abuse my kindness. And I will lock myself up in the most merciful Heart of Jesus. I will bear my own suffering in silence. May Your mercy, O Lord, rest upon me.

—St. Faustina, *Diary*, 163

My Adoration Prayers

My Adoration Prayers

My Adoration Prayers

PRAYERS FOR VARIOUS OCCASIONS

"More things are wrought by prayer
than this world dreams of.
Wherefore, let thy voice rise like a
fountain for me night and day.
For what are men better than sheep
or goats that nourish a blind life
within the brain if, knowing God,
they lift not hands of prayer
both for themselves
and those who call them friends?
For so the whole round earth
is every way bound by gold chains
about the feet of God."

—Tennyson, *Idylls of the King*

PRAYERS, LITANIES, AND NOVENAS

*"Lord, open my lips, and my mouth
will proclaim Your praise."*

—From the Divine Office: The Invitatory

DAILY OFFERING

LORD, Jesus, You lived and died for me. Help me to keep that thought before me today, so that whatever life brings, whether it be success or failure, satisfaction or disappointment, happiness or sorrow, I may offer it to You. Through me, may everyone I meet this day see You, Lord, feel Your presence, and experience Your love. Lord, I offer You today. May I serve You by serving others in Your Name, making all that I do a gift of love and thanksgiving for all You have done for me.

UNIVERSAL PRAYER ATTRIBUTED TO POPE ST. CLEMENT

LORD, I believe in You: increase my faith.
I trust in You: strengthen my trust.
I love You: let me love You more and more.
I am sorry for my sins: deepen my sorrow.
I worship You as my first beginning,
I long for You as my last end,
I praise You as my constant helper,
And call on You as my loving protector.
Guide me by Your wisdom,
Correct me with Your justice,
Comfort me with Your mercy,
Protect me with Your power.
I offer You, Lord, my thoughts: to be fixed on You;
My words: to have You for their theme;
My actions: to reflect my love for You and follow
Your will;
My sufferings: to be endured for Your greater glory.
I want to do what You ask of me:
In the way You ask,
For as long as You ask,
Because You ask.
Lord, enlighten my understanding,
Strengthen my will,
Purify my heart, and make me holy.

Help me to repent of my past sins
And to resist temptation in the future.
Help me to rise above my human weaknesses
And cultivate the virtues I should have.
Let me love You, my Lord and my God,
And see myself as I really am:
A pilgrim in this world,
A Christian called to respect and love
All whose lives I touch,
Those under my authority,
My friends and my enemies.
Help me to conquer anger with gentleness,
Pleasure-seeking by self-denial,
Greed by generosity, Apathy by fervor.
Help me to forget myself
And reach out toward others.

Make me prudent in planning,
Courageous in times of danger,
Patient in suffering,
And unassuming in prosperity.
Keep me, Lord, attentive at prayer,
Temperate in food and drink,
Diligent in my work,
Firm in my good intentions.
Let my conscience be clear,
My conduct without fault,

My speech blameless,
My life well-ordered.
Put me on guard
against my human weaknesses,
Help me to master my natural impulses,
Let me cherish Your love for me,
Keep Your law,
And come at last to Your salvation.
Teach me to realize that this world is passing,
That my true future is the happiness of heaven,
That life on earth is short,
And the life to come eternal.
Help me to live my life,
With a proper fear of judgment,
But a greater trust in Your goodness.
Lead me safely through death
To the endless joy of heaven.
Grant this through Christ our Lord.

—Adapted from the Roman Missal,
Seventh Edition

St. Patrick's Breastplate

I arise today
Through a mighty strength,
the invocation of the Trinity,
Through belief in the Threeness,
Through confession of the Oneness
of the Creator of creation.

I arise today
Through the strength of Christ's birth
with His baptism,
Through the strength of His crucifixion
with His burial,
Through the strength of His
resurrection with His ascension,
Through the strength of His descent
for the judgment of doom.

I arise today
Through the strength of the
love of cherubim,
In the obedience of angels,
In the service of archangels,
In the hope of resurrection
to meet with reward,
In the prayers of patriarchs,
In the predictions of prophets,

In the preaching of apostles,
In the faith of confessors,
In the innocence of holy virgins,
In the deeds of righteous men.

I arise today, through
The strength of heaven,
The light of the sun,
The radiance of the moon,
The splendor of fire,
The speed of lightning,
The swiftness of wind,
The depth of the sea,
The stability of the earth,
The firmness of rock.

I arise today, through
God's strength to pilot me,
God's might to uphold me,
God's wisdom to guide me,
God's eye to look before me,
God's ear to hear me,
God's word to speak for me,
God's hand to guard me,
God's shield to protect me,
God's host to save me
From snares of devils,
From temptation of vices,

From everyone who shall wish me ill,
afar and near.

I summon today
All these powers between me and those evils,
Against every cruel and merciless power
that may oppose my body and soul,
Against incantations of false prophets,
Against black laws of pagandom,
Against false laws of heretics,
Against craft of idolatry,
Against spells of witches and smiths and wizards,
Against every knowledge
that corrupts man's body and soul;
Christ to shield me today
Against poison, against burning,
Against drowning, against wounding,
So that there may come to me
an abundance of reward.
Christ with me,
Christ before me,
Christ behind me,
Christ in me,
Christ beneath me,
Christ above me,
Christ on my right,
Christ on my left,

Christ when I lie down,
Christ when I sit down,
Christ when I arise,
Christ in the heart of everyone who thinks of me,
Christ in the mouth of everyone who speaks of me,
Christ in every eye that sees me,
Christ in every ear that hears me.

I arise today
Through a mighty strength,
the invocation of the Trinity,
Through belief in the Threeness,
Through confession of the Oneness
of the Creator of creation.

CARDINAL MERCIER'S SECRET OF SANCTITY

I AM going to reveal to you the secret of sanctity and happiness. Every day for five minutes control your imagination and close your eyes to all the noises of the world in order to enter into yourself. Then, in the sanctuary of your baptized soul (which is the temple of the Holy Spirit) speak to that Divine Spirit, saying to Him:

O Holy Spirit, soul of my soul, I adore You. Enlighten, guide, strengthen, and console me. Tell me what I

ought to do and command me to do it. I promise to be
submissive in everything You permit to happen to me.
Only show me what is Your will.

If you do this, your life will flow along happily, serenely, and full of consolation, even in the midst of trials. Grace will be proportioned to the trial, giving you the strength to carry it and you will arrive at the Gate of Paradise, laden with merit. This submission to the Holy Spirit is the secret of sanctity.

Novena of Surrender

Fr. Dolindo Ruotolo

Day 1

WHY do you confuse yourselves by worrying? Leave the care of your affairs to me and everything will be peaceful. I say to you in truth that every act of true, blind, complete surrender to me produces the effect that you desire and resolves all difficult situations.

O Jesus, I surrender myself to You. Take care of
everything! (10 times)

Day 2

SURRENDER to me does not mean to fret, to be upset, or to lose hope; nor does it mean offering to me a worried prayer asking me to follow you and change your worry into prayer. It is against this surrender, deeply against it, to worry, to be nervous and to desire to think about the consequences of anything. It is like the confusion that children feel when they ask their mother to see to their needs, and then try to take care of those needs for themselves, so that their childlike efforts get in their mother's way.

Surrender means to placidly close the eyes of the soul, to turn away from thoughts of tribulation and to put yourself in my care, so that only I act, saying "You take care of it."

O Jesus, I surrender myself to You. Take care of everything! (10 times)

Day 3

HOW many things I do when the soul, in so much spiritual and material need turns to me, looks at me and says to me: "You take care of it," then closes its eyes and rests. In pain you pray for me to act, but that I act in the way you want. You do not turn to me; instead, you want me to adapt to your ideas. You are not sick people who ask the doctor to cure you, but rather sick people who tell the doctor how to. So do not act this way, but pray as I taught you in the Our Father: "Hallowed be thy Name"; that is, be glorified in my need. "Thy kingdom come"; that is, let all that is in us and in the world be in accord with Your kingdom. "Thy will be done on Earth as it is in Heaven"; that is, in our need, decide as You see fit for our temporal and eternal life.

If you say to me truly: "Thy will be done" (which is the same as saying: "You take care of it"), I will intervene with all my omnipotence, and I will resolve the most difficult situations.

O Jesus, I surrender myself to You. Take care of everything! (10 times)

Day 4

YOU see evil growing instead of weakening? Do not worry. Close Your eyes and say to me with faith: "Thy will be done. You take care of it." I say to you that I will take care of it, and that I will intervene as does a doctor, and I will accomplish miracles when they are needed. Do you see that the sick person is getting worse? Do not be upset, but close your eyes and say, "You take care of it." I say to you that I will take care of it, and that there is no medicine more powerful than my loving intervention. By my love, I promise this to you.

O Jesus, I surrender myself to You. Take care of everything! (10 times)

Day 5

AND when I must lead you on a path different from the one you see, I will prepare you; I will carry you in my arms; I will let you find yourself, like children who have fallen asleep in their mother's arms, on the other bank of the river. What troubles you and hurts you immensely are your reason, your thoughts and worry, and your desire at all costs to deal with what afflicts you.

O Jesus, I surrender myself to You. Take care of everything! (10 times)

Day 6

YOU are sleepless; you want to judge every-thing, direct everything, and see to every-thing; and you surrender to human strength, or worse, to men themselves, trusting in their intervention—this is what hinders my words and my views. O how much I wish from you this sur-render, to help you; and how I suffer when I see you so agitated! Satan tries to do exactly this: to agitate you, to remove you from my protection, and to throw you into the jaws of human initia-tive. So, trust only in me, rest in me, surrender to me in everything.

O Jesus, I surrender myself to You. Take care of everything! (10 times)

Day 7

I PERFORM miracles in proportion to your full surrender to me and to your not think-ing of yourselves. I sow treasure troves of graces when you are in the deepest poverty. No person of reason, no thinker, has ever performed mira-cles, not even among the saints. He does divine works whosoever surrenders to God. So don't think about it any more, because your mind is acute and for you it is very hard to see evil, to trust in me, and to not think of yourself. Do this for all your needs, do this all of you, and you will see great continual silent miracles. I will take care of things. I promise this to you.

O Jesus, I surrender myself to You. Take care of everything! (10 times)

Day 8

CLOSE your eyes and let yourself be carried away on the flowing current of my grace; close your eyes and do not think of the present, turning your thoughts away from the future just as you would from temptation. Repose in me, believing in my goodness, and I promise you by my love that, if you say, "You take care of it," I will take care of it all. I will console you, liberate you, and guide you.

O Jesus, I surrender myself to You. Take care of everything! (10 times)

Day 9

PRAY always in readiness to surrender, and you will receive from it great peace and great rewards, even when I confer on you the grace of immolation, of repentance, and of love. Then what does suffering matter? It seems impossible to you? Close your eyes and say with all your soul, "Jesus, you take care of it." Do not be afraid, I will take care of things, and you will bless my name by humbling yourself. A thousand prayers cannot equal one single act of surrender; remember this well. There is no novena more effective than this: "O Jesus, I surrender myself to You."

O Jesus, I surrender myself to You. Take care of everything! (10 times)

LITANY OF HUMILITY

O JESUS! meek and humble of heart,
Make my heart like Yours.

R: *Deliver me, Jesus.*

From self-will,
From the desire of being esteemed,
From the desire of being loved,
From the desire of being extolled,
From the desire of being honored,
From the desire of being praised,
From the desire of being preferred to others,
From the desire of being consulted,
From the desire of being approved,
From the desire of being understood,
From the desire of being visited,
From the fear of being humiliated,
From the fear of being despised,
From the fear of being rebuked,
From the fear of being slandered,
From the fear of being forgotten,
From the fear of being ridiculed,
From the fear of being suspected,
From the fear of being wronged,
From the fear of being abandoned,
From the fear of being refused,

R: Jesus, grant me the grace to desire it.
That others may be loved more than I,
That others may be esteemed more than I,
That, in the opinion of the world, others may
    increase and I may decrease,
That others may be chosen and I set aside,
That others may be praised and I unnoticed,
That others may be preferred to me in everything,
That others may become holier than I, provided
    that I may become as holy as I should,

R: Lord, I want to rejoice.
At being unknown and poor,
At being deprived of the natural perfections of
    body and mind,
When people do not think of me,
When they assign to me the meanest tasks,
When they do not even deign to make use
    of me,
When they never ask my opinion,
When they leave me at the lowest place,
When they never compliment me,
When they blame me in season and out of
    season,

Blessed are those who suffer persecution for
    justice's sake,
    For theirs is the kingdom of heaven.

—Adapted from Rafael Cardinal Merry del Val[42]

LITANY OF THE MOST PRECIOUS BLOOD OF JESUS

LORD, have mercy. *Lord have mercy.*
Christ, have mercy. *Christ have mercy.*
Lord, have mercy. *Lord have mercy.*
Jesus, hear us. *Jesus, graciously hear us.*

R: *Have mercy on us.*
God, the Father of Heaven,
God, the Son, Redeemer of the world,
God, the Holy Spirit,
Holy Trinity, One God,

R: *Save us.*
Blood of Christ, only-begotten Son of the
     Eternal Father,
Blood of Christ, Incarnate Word of God,
Blood of Christ, of the New and Eternal
     Testament,
Blood of Christ, falling upon the earth in the
     Agony,
Blood of Christ, shed profusely in the
     Scourging,
Blood of Christ, flowing forth in the Crowning
     with Thorns,
Blood of Christ, poured out on the Cross,
Blood of Christ, price of our salvation,

Blood of Christ, without which there is no
forgiveness,

Blood of Christ, Eucharistic drink and
refreshment of souls,

Blood of Christ, stream of mercy,

Blood of Christ, victor over demons,

Blood of Christ, courage of Martyrs,

Blood of Christ, strength of Confessors,

Blood of Christ, bringing forth Virgins,

Blood of Christ, help of those in peril,

Blood of Christ, relief of the burdened,

Blood of Christ, solace in sorrow,

Blood of Christ, hope of the penitent,

Blood of Christ, consolation of the dying,

Blood of Christ, peace and tenderness of hearts,

Blood of Christ, pledge of eternal life,

Blood of Christ, freeing souls from purgatory,

Blood of Christ, most worthy of all glory and
honor,

Lamb of God, who take away the sins of the
world, *spare us, O Lord.*

Lamb of God, who take away the sins of the
world, *graciously hear us, O Lord.*

Lamb of God, who take away the sins of the
world, *have mercy on us.*

You have redeemed us, O Lord, in Your Blood.

And made us, for our God, a kingdom.

Let us pray:

Almighty and eternal God, You have appointed Your only-begotten Son the Redeemer of the world, and willed to be appeased by His Blood. Grant we beg of You, that we may worthily adore this price of our salvation, and through its power be safeguarded from the evils of the present life, so that we may rejoice in its fruits forever in heaven. Through the same Christ our Lord. Amen.

LITANY OF LORETO

LORD have mercy.
Christ have mercy.
Lord have mercy. Christ hear us.
Christ graciously hear us.
God, the Father of heaven,
have mercy on us.
God the Son, Redeemer of the world,
have mercy on us.
God the Holy Spirit,
have mercy on us.
Holy Trinity, one God,
have mercy on us.

R: Pray for us.

Holy Mary,
Holy Mother of God,
Holy Virgin of virgins,
Mother of Christ,
Mother of the Church,
Mother of divine grace,
Mother most pure,
Mother most chaste,
Mother inviolate,
Mother undefiled,
Mother most amiable,
Mother admirable,
Mother of good counsel,
Mother of our Creator,
Mother of our Saviour,
Mother of mercy,
Virgin most prudent,
Virgin most venerable,
Virgin most renowned,
Virgin most powerful,
Virgin most merciful,
Virgin most faithful,
Mirror of justice,
Seat of wisdom,
Cause of our joy,
Spiritual vessel,

Vessel of honour,
Singular vessel of devotion,
Mystical rose,
Tower of David,
Tower of ivory,
House of gold,
Ark of the covenant,
Gate of heaven,
Morning star,
Health of the sick,
Refuge of sinners,
Comfort of the afflicted,
Help of Christians,
Queen of Angels,
Queen of Patriarchs,
Queen of Prophets,
Queen of Apostles,
Queen of Martyrs,
Queen of Confessors,
Queen of Virgins,
Queen of all Saints,
Queen conceived without original sin,
Queen assumed into heaven,
Queen of the most holy Rosary,
Queen of families,
Queen of peace,

Lamb of God, who take away the sins of the world, *spare us, O Lord.*

Lamb of God, who take away the sins of the world, *graciously hear us, O Lord.*

Lamb of God, who take away the sins of the world, *have mercy on us.*

Pray for us, O holy Mother of God.

That we may be made worthy of the promises of Christ.

Let us pray.

Grant, we beseech You, O Lord God, that we, Your servants, may enjoy perpetual health of mind and body; and by the intercession of the Blessed Mary, ever Virgin, may be delivered from present sorrow, and obtain eternal joy. Through Christ our Lord. Amen.

LITANY OF PRESENCE

Fr. George Kosicki, CSB

R: Jesus, You are present!

Jesus, You are here in the Eucharist,
As Son of the Father and Son of Mary,
As the Word made flesh (Lk 1; Jn 1),
By word and the Spirit (Jn 3),
As Mercy Incarnate (Pope John Paul II),
Because You love us (Jn 13:11),
As the Lamb of God (Jn 1:29),
As totally given and outpoured (Lk 22:19),
As the New Covenant (Jn 6:27, Lk 22:20),
Body, Blood, Soul, and Divinity,
As the Memorial of Your passion, death and
    resurrection (Canon of the Mass),
As the remembrance of all You have done for us
    (1 Cor 11:25),
As thanksgiving to the Father (Mt 26:27),
As sacrificial Gift to the Father (Heb 10:10),
As the Promise of resurrection (see 1 Cor 11:30),
To give us eternal life (Jn 6:51–58),
To nourish us (Jn 6:54),
As Icon of the invisible God (Col 1:15),
Though hidden like the Father,
As a Pleasing Aroma to the Father (see 2 Cor
    2:15),

As Priest, Prophet, and King,
As the Holy One, the Humble One, the Merciful
     One,
In all past and future,
As the pledge of Your coming again (see 1 Cor
     11:26),
As the Bridegroom longing for communion (Lk
     22:15),
As the Mystery of Faith,
As the Mystery of Mercy,
As the Hope of Glory,
Jesus, You are here and You call us (Jn 11:28),

LITANY OF ST. JOSEPH

LORD, have mercy. *Lord have mercy.*
Christ, have mercy. *Christ have mercy.*
Lord, have mercy. *Lord have mercy.*
Christ, hear us. *Christ, graciously hear us.*

God the Father of Heaven,
Have mercy on us.
God the Son, Redeemer of the world,
Have mercy on us.
God the Holy Spirit,
Have mercy on us.
Holy Trinity, One God,
Have mercy on us.

R: Pray for us.
Holy Mary,
Saint Joseph,
Illustrious son of David,
Light of the patriarchs,
Spouse of the Mother of God,
Chaste guardian of the Virgin,
Foster-father of the Son of God,
Watchful defender of Christ,
Head of the Holy Family,
Joseph most just,

Joseph most chaste,
Joseph most prudent,
Joseph most valiant,
Joseph most obedient,
Joseph most faithful,
Mirror of patience,
Lover of poverty,
Model of workmen,
Glory of domestic life,
Guardian of virgins,
Pillar of families,
Solace of the afflicted,
Hope of the sick,
Patron of the dying,
Terror of demons,
Protector of Holy Church,

Lamb of God, Who take away the sins of the
     world, *spare us, O Lord.*
Lamb of God, Who take away the sins of the
     world, *graciously hear us, O Lord.*
Lamb of God, Who take away the sins of the
     world, *have mercy on us.*

V. He made Him the lord of His household,
R. *And prince over all His possessions.*

Let us pray.

O God, in Your ineffable providence You were pleased to choose Blessed Joseph to be the spouse of Your most Holy Mother; grant, we beg You, that we may be worthy to have Him for our intercessor in heaven whom on earth we venerate as our Protector: You who live and reign forever and ever. R. Amen.

LITANY OF THE SACRED HEART OF JESUS

LORD, have mercy. *Lord, have mercy.*
Christ, have mercy. *Christ, have mercy.*
Lord, have mercy. *Lord, have mercy.*
Christ, hear us. *Christ, graciously hear us.*

R: *Have mercy on us.*

God the Father of Heaven,
God the Son, Redeemer of the world,
God, the Holy Spirit,
Holy Trinity, One God,
Heart of Jesus, Son of the Eternal Father,
Heart of Jesus, formed by the Holy Spirit in the
     womb of the Virgin Mother,
Heart of Jesus, substantially united to the Word
     of God,
Heart of Jesus, of Infinite Majesty,

Heart of Jesus, Sacred Temple of God,

Heart of Jesus, Tabernacle of the Most High,

Heart of Jesus, House of God and Gate of
Heaven,

Heart of Jesus, burning furnace of charity,

Heart of Jesus, abode of justice and love,

Heart of Jesus, full of goodness and love,

Heart of Jesus, abyss of all virtues,

Heart of Jesus, most worthy of all praise,

Heart of Jesus, in whom are all treasures of
wisdom and knowledge,

Heart of Jesus, in whom dwells the fullness of
divinity,

Heart of Jesus, in whom the Father was well
pleased,

Heart of Jesus, of whose fullness we have all
received,

Heart of Jesus, desire of the everlasting hills,

Heart of Jesus, patient and most merciful,

Heart of Jesus, enriching all who invoke Thee,

Heart of Jesus, fountain of life and holiness,

Heart of Jesus, propitiation for our sins,

Heart of Jesus, loaded down with opprobrium,

Heart of Jesus, bruised for our offenses,

Heart of Jesus, obedient to death,

Heart of Jesus, pierced with a lance,

Heart of Jesus, source of all consolation,

Heart of Jesus, our life and resurrection,

Heart of Jesus, our peace and our reconciliation,
Heart of Jesus, victim for our sins,
Heart of Jesus, salvation of those who trust in
       Thee,
Heart of Jesus, hope of those who die in Thee,
Heart of Jesus, delight of all the Saints,

Lamb of God, who take away the sins of the
       world, *spare us, O Lord.*
Lamb of God, who take away the sins of the
       world, *graciously hear us, O Lord.*
Lamb of God, who take away the sins of the
       world, *have mercy on us, O Lord.*
Jesus, meek and humble of heart,
Make our hearts like to Thine.

Let us pray.
   Almighty and eternal God, look upon the
Heart of Thy most beloved Son and upon the
praises and satisfaction which He offers Thee in
the name of sinners; and to those who implore
Thy mercy, in Thy great goodness, grant forgiveness in the name of the same Jesus Christ, Thy
Son, who lives and reign with Thee forever and
ever. Amen.

Litany of the Most Holy Name of Jesus

LORD, have mercy.
Christ, have mercy.
Lord, have mercy, Jesus, hear us.
Jesus, graciously hear us.

R. Have mercy on us.
God the Father of Heaven,
God the Son, Redeemer of the world,
God the Holy Spirit,
Holy Trinity, One God,
Jesus, Son of the living God,
Jesus, Splendor of the Father,
Jesus, Brightness of eternal Light,
Jesus, King of Glory,
Jesus, Sun of Justice,
Jesus, Son of the Virgin Mary,
Jesus, most amiable,
Jesus, most admirable,
Jesus, the mighty God,
Jesus, Father of the world to come,
Jesus, angel of great counsel,
Jesus, most powerful,
Jesus, most patient,
Jesus, most obedient,
Jesus, meek and humble of heart,

Jesus, Lover of Chastity,
Jesus, our Lover,
Jesus, God of Peace,
Jesus, Author of Life,
Jesus, Model of Virtues,
Jesus, zealous for souls,
Jesus, our God,
Jesus, our Refuge,
Jesus, Father of the Poor
Jesus, Treasure of the Faithful,
Jesus, good Shepherd,
Jesus, true Light,
Jesus, eternal Wisdom,
Jesus, infinite Goodness,
Jesus, our Way and our Life,
Jesus, Joy of the Angels,
Jesus, King of the Patriarchs,
Jesus, Master of the Apostles,
Jesus, Teacher of the Evangelists,
Jesus, Strength of Martyrs,
Jesus, Light of Confessors,
Jesus, Purity of Virgins,
Jesus, Crown of all Saints,

Be merciful. *Spare us, O Jesus.*
Be merciful. *Graciously hear us, O Jesus.*

R. Deliver us, O Jesus.

From all evil,

From all sin,

From Your wrath,

From the snares of the devil,

From the spirit of fornication,

From everlasting death,

From the neglect of Your inspirations,

Through the mystery of Your Holy Incarnation,

Through Your Nativity,

Through Your Infancy,

Through Your most divine Life,

Through Your Labors,

Through Your Agony and Passion,

Through Your Cross and Dereliction,

Through Your Sufferings,

Through Your Death and Burial,

Through Your Resurrection,

Through Your Ascension,

Through Your Institution of the Most Holy
     Eucharist,

Through Your Joys,

Through Your Glory,

Lamb of God, Who take away the sins of the world, *spare us, O Jesus!*

Lamb of God, Who take away the sins of the world, *graciously hear us, O Jesus!*

Lamb of God, Who take away the sins of the world, *have mercy on us, O Jesus!*

Let us pray.

"Ask and you shall receive; seek and you shall find; knock and it shall be opened to you." Mercifully attend to our supplications, and grant us the gift of Your most divine love, that we may love You with all our hearts, and in all our words and actions, and never cease to praise You.

Make us, O Lord, to have a perpetual fear and love of Your holy name, for You never fail to govern those whom You establish in Your love. You, Who live and reign forever and ever. Amen.

DIVINE MERCY LITANY

From the Diary of St. Faustina (949)

Divine Mercy, gushing forth from the bosom of the Father, I trust in You.

Divine Mercy, greatest attribute of God, I trust in You.

Divine Mercy, incomprehensible mystery, I trust in You.

Divine Mercy, fountain gushing forth from the mystery of the Most Blessed Trinity, I trust in You.

Divine Mercy, unfathomed by any intellect, human or angelic, I trust in You.

Divine Mercy, from which wells forth all life and happiness, I trust in You.

Divine Mercy, better than the heavens, I trust in You.

Divine Mercy, source of miracles and wonders, I trust in You.

Divine Mercy, encompassing the whole universe, I trust in You.

Divine Mercy, descending to earth in the Person of the Incarnate Word, I trust in You.

Divine Mercy, which flowed out from the open wound of the Heart of Jesus, I trust in You.

Divine Mercy, enclosed in the Heart of Jesus for us, and especially for sinners, I trust in You.

Divine Mercy, unfathomed in the institution of the Sacred Host, I trust in You.

Divine Mercy, in the founding of the Holy Church, I trust in You.

Divine Mercy, in the Sacrament of Holy Baptism, I trust in You.

Divine Mercy, in our justification through Jesus Christ, I trust in You.

Divine Mercy, accompanying us through our whole life, I trust in You.

Divine Mercy, embracing us especially at the hour of death, I trust in You.

Divine Mercy, endowing us with immortal life, I trust in You.

Divine Mercy, accompanying us every moment of our life, I trust in You.

Divine Mercy, shielding us from the fire of hell, I trust in You.

Divine Mercy, in the conversion of hardened sinners, I trust in You.

Divine Mercy, astonishment for Angels, incomprehensible to Saints, I trust in You.

Divine Mercy, unfathomed in all the mysteries of God, I trust in You.

Divine Mercy, lifting us out of every misery, I trust in You.

Divine Mercy, source of our happiness and joy, I trust in You.

Divine Mercy, in calling us forth from
nothingness to existence, I trust in You.

Divine Mercy, embracing all the works of His
hands, I trust in You.

Divine Mercy, crown of all God's handiwork, I
trust in You.

Divine Mercy, in which we are all immersed, I
trust in You.

Divine Mercy, sweet relief for anguished hearts,
I trust in You.

Divine Mercy, only hope of despairing souls, I
trust in You.

Divine Mercy, repose of hearts, peace amidst
fear, I trust in You.

Divine Mercy, delight and ecstasy of holy souls, I
trust in You.

Divine Mercy, inspiring hope against all hope, I
trust in You.

Prayer:

Eternal God, in whom mercy is endless and
the treasury of compassion inexhaustible, look
kindly upon us and increase Your mercy in us,
that in difficult moments we might not despair
nor become despondent, but with great confidence submit ourselves to Your holy will, which
is Love and Mercy itself.

LITANY OF THE MOST BLESSED SACRAMENT

St. Peter Julian Eymard

L ORD, have mercy on us.
Lord have mercy on us.
Christ, have mercy on us.
Christ have mercy on us.
Lord, have mercy on us.
Lord have mercy on us.
Christ, hear us.
Christ, graciously hear us.

R. Have mercy on us.

God the Father of Heaven,
God the Son, Redeemer of the world,
God the Holy Spirit,
Holy Trinity, One God,
Jesus, Eternal High Priest of the Eucharistic
    Sacrifice,
Jesus, Divine Victim on the Altar for our
    salvation,
Jesus, hidden under the appearance of bread,
Jesus, dwelling in the tabernacles of the world,
Jesus, really, truly and substantially present in
    the Blessed Sacrament,

Jesus, abiding in Your fullness, Body, Blood,
    Soul and Divinity,

Jesus, Bread of Life,

Jesus, Bread of Angels,

Jesus, with us always until the end of the world,

Sacred Host, summit and source of all worship
    and Christian life,

Sacred Host, sign and cause of the unity of the
    Church,

Sacred Host, adored by countless angels,

Sacred Host, spiritual food,

Sacred Host, Sacrament of love,

Sacred Host, bond of charity,

Sacred Host, greatest aid to holiness,

Sacred Host, gift and glory of the priesthood,

Sacred Host, in which we partake of Christ,

Sacred Host, in which the soul is filled with
    grace,

Sacred Host, in which we are given a pledge of
    future glory,

Blessed be Jesus in the Most Holy Sacrament of
    the Altar.

Blessed be Jesus in the Most Holy Sacrament of
    the Altar.

Blessed be Jesus in the Most Holy Sacrament of
    the Altar.

For those who do not believe in Your Eucharistic
   presence, *Have mercy, O Lord.*
For those who are indifferent to the Sacrament
   of Your love, *Have mercy on us.*
For those who have offended You in the Holy
   Sacrament of the Altar, *Have mercy on us.*

R. *We beseech You, hear us.*

That we may show fitting reverence when
   entering Your holy temple,
That we may make suitable preparation before
   approaching the Altar,
That we may receive You frequently in Holy
   Communion with real devotion and true
   humility,
That we may never neglect to thank You for so
   wonderful a blessing,
That we may cherish time spent in silent prayer
   before You,
That we may grow in knowledge of this
   Sacrament of sacraments,
That all priests may have a profound love of the
   Holy Eucharist,
That they may celebrate the Holy Sacrifice of the
   Mass in accordance with its sublime dignity,
That we may be comforted and sanctified with
   Holy Viaticum at the hour of our death,

That we may see You one day face to face in
Heaven,

Lamb of God, You take away the sins of the
world, *spare us, O Lord.*
Lamb of God, You take away the sins of the
world, *spare us, O Lord.*
Lamb of God, You take away the sins of the
world, *spare us, O Lord.*
O Sacrament Most Holy, O Sacrament Divine,
All praise and all thanksgiving be every
moment Thine.

Let us pray.

Most merciful Father, You continue to draw
us to Yourself through the Eucharistic Mystery.
Grant us fervent faith in this Sacrament of love,
in which Christ the Lord Himself is contained,
offered, and received. We make this prayer
through the same Christ our Lord. Amen.

NOVENA TO MARY UNDOER OF KNOTS

Introduction to the Novena

From a reflection by Pope Francis on Mary, the Untier of Knots, October 15, 2013.

MARY'S faith unties the knot of sin (cf. Lumen Gentium, 56). What does that mean? The Fathers of the Second Vatican Council took up a phrase of Saint Irenaeus, who states that "the knot of Eve's disobedience was untied by the obedience of Mary; what the virgin Eve bound by her unbelief, the Virgin Mary loosened by her faith" (*Adversus Haereses*, III, 22, 4).

. . . We know one thing: nothing is impossible for God's mercy! Even the most tangled knots are loosened by his grace.

What are the knots in my life? "Father, my knots cannot be undone!" It is a mistake to say anything of the sort! All the knots of our heart, every knot of our conscience, can be undone.

The Novena to Mary Undoer of Knots

Sign of the Cross
Act of Contrition
First three decades of the Rosary
Meditation of the day

Last two decades of the Rosary
Closing Prayer to Mary, Undoer of Knots
Sign of the Cross

Prayer to Mary Undoer of Knots

(Closing Prayer Each Day)

VIRGIN Mary, Mother of fair love, Mother who never refuses to come to the aid of a child in need, Mother whose hands never cease to serve your beloved children, because they are moved by the divine love and immense mercy that exists in your heart, cast your compassionate eyes upon me and see the snarl of knots that exist in my life. You know very well how desperate I am, my pain, and how I am bound by these knots. Mary, Mother to whom God entrusted the undoing of the knots in the lives of His children, I entrust into your hands the ribbon of my life. No one, not even the Evil One himself, can take it away from your precious care. In your hands there is no knot that cannot be undone. Powerful Mother, by your grace and intercessory power with Your Son and My Liberator, Jesus, take into your hands today this knot. [Mention your request here]

I beg you to undo it for the glory of God, once for all. You are my hope. O my Lady, you are

the abiding consolation God gives me, the for-
tification of my feeble strength, the enrichment
of my destitution, and, with Christ, the freedom
from my chains. Hear my plea. Keep me, guide
me, protect me, o safe refuge!

Mary, Undoer of Knots, pray for me.

Day 1

*On the first day of the novena, we acknowledge the vari-
ous knots in our life and the suffering they cause, and ask
the Blessed Virgin to tenderly begin to undo them out of
her maternal love for us.*

Meditation for the First Day

DEAREST Holy Mother, Most Holy Mary, you
undo the knots that suffocate your children,
extend your merciful hands to me. I entrust to
you today this knot [*Mention your request here*] and
all the negative consequences that it provokes
in my life. I give you this knot that torments me
and makes me unhappy and so impedes me from
uniting myself to you and your Son, Jesus, my
Savior.

I run to you, Mary, Undoer of Knots because
I trust you and I know that you never despise a
sinning child who comes to ask you for help. I
believe that you can undo this knot because Jesus

grants you everything. I believe that you want
to undo this knot because you are my Mother. I
believe that you will do this because you love me
with eternal love. Thank you, Dear Mother.

Mary, Undoer of Knots, pray for me.

Day 2

*On the second day of the novena, we ask the Blessed Vir-
gin to intercede with Christ for us, that we may abandon
our sinful life and take up the virtues that help us to grow
in the image and likeness of God.*

Meditation for the Second Day

MARY, Beloved Mother, channel of all grace,
I return to you today my heart, recognizing
that I am a sinner in need of your help. Many times
I lose the graces you grant me because of my sins
of egoism, pride, rancor and my lack of generosity
and humility. I turn to you today, Mary, Undoer
of Knots, for you to ask your Son Jesus to grant
me a pure, divested, humble and trusting heart.
I will live today practicing these virtues and offering you this as a sign of my love for you. I entrust
into your hands this knot [mention your request here]
which keeps me from reflecting the glory of God.

Mary, Undoer of Knots, pray for me.

Day 3

On the third day of the novena, we acknowledge that the knots in our life are often self-made, even when they appear to be caused by others. Our actions provoke others, who provoke us, which leads us to anger and resentment against those we have provoked. The very description of the circumstances sounds like the tying of a knot!

Meditation for the Third Day

MEDIATING Mother, Queen of heaven, in whose hands the treasures of the King are found, turn your merciful eyes upon me today. I entrust into your holy hands this knot in my life [mention your request here] and all the rancor and resentment it has caused in me. I ask Your forgiveness, God the Father, for my sin. Help me now to forgive all the persons who consciously or unconsciously provoked this knot. Give me, also, the grace to forgive me for having provoked this knot. Only in this way can You undo it. Before you, dearest Mother, and in the name of your Son, Jesus, my Savior, who has suffered so many offenses, having been granted forgiveness, I now forgive these persons [mention their names here] and myself, forever. Thank you, Mary, Undoer of Knots for undoing the knot of rancor in my heart and the knot which I now present to you. Amen.

Mary, Undoer of Knots, pray for me.

Day 4

On the fourth day of the novena, we pray for the strength to overcome our spiritual paralysis, which prevents us from working through the knots in our spiritual life.

Meditation for the Fourth Day

DEAREST Holy Mother, you are generous with all who seek you, have mercy on me. I entrust into your hands this knot which robs the peace of my heart, paralyzes my soul and keeps me from going to my Lord and serving Him with my life. Undo this knot in my love [mention your request here], O Mother, and ask Jesus to heal my paralytic faith, which gets downhearted with the stones on the road. Along with you, dearest Mother, may I see these stones as friends. Not murmuring against them anymore but giving endless thanks for them, may I smile trustingly in your power.

Mary, Undoer of Knots, pray for me.

Day 5

On the fifth day of the novena, we ask Mary to intercede for us, that Christ may send His Holy Spirit upon us. Just as the Blessed Virgin and the Apostles were filled with the Holy Spirit on Pentecost Sunday, changing their lives forever, we hope to abandon all of our vices and embrace the gifts of the Holy Spirit.

Meditation for the Fifth Day

MOTHER, Undoer of Knots, generous and compassionate, I come to you today to once again entrust this knot [mention your request here] in my life to you and to ask the divine wisdom to undo, under the light of the Holy Spirit, this snarl of problems. No one ever saw you angry; to the contrary, your words were so charged with sweetness that the Holy Spirit was manifested on your lips. Take away from me the bitterness, anger, and hatred which this knot has caused me. Give me, O dearest Mother, some of the sweetness and wisdom that is all silently reflected in your heart. And just as you were present at Pentecost, ask Jesus to send me a new presence of the Holy Spirit at this moment in my life. Holy Spirit, come upon me!

Mary, Undoer of Knots, pray for me.

Day 6

On the sixth day of the novena, we acknowledge that God will answer our prayers in His time, not ours; and we ask Mary to intercede for us that we may have the patience to wait. At the same time, we acknowledge that we have our part to play, as well, in receiving the Sacrament of Holy Communion and the Sacrament of Confession, so that when our prayers are answered, we may have the grace to receive the answer with gratitude and thanksgiving.

Meditation for the Sixth Day

QUEEN of Mercy, I entrust to you this knot in my life [mention your request here] and I ask you to give me a heart that is patient until you undo it. Teach me to persevere in the living word of Jesus, in the Eucharist, the Sacrament of Confession; stay with me and prepare my heart to celebrate with the angels the grace that will be granted to me. Amen! Alleluia!

Mary, Undoer of Knots, pray for me.

Day 7

On the seventh day of the novena, the meditation recalls the icon of Mary Undoer of Knots, in which the Blessed Virgin, the Second Eve, crushes the head of the serpent beneath her heel. Freed from the power of demons, we reaffirm our allegiance to Christ.

Meditation for the Seventh Day

MOTHER Most Pure, I come to you today to beg you to undo this knot in my life [mention your request here] and free me from the snares of evil. God has granted you great power over all the demons. I renounce all of them today, every connection I have had with them, and I proclaim Jesus as my one and only Lord and Savior. Mary, Undoer of Knots, crush the Evil One's head and destroy the traps he has set for me by this knot. Thank you, dearest Mother. Most Precious Blood of Jesus, free me!

Mary, Undoer of Knots, pray for me.

Day 8

On the eighth day of the novena, the meditation recalls the Visitation, when the Blessed Virgin, awash in the joy of the Annunciation, went to minister to her cousin Elizabeth, who was pregnant with John the Baptist. Filled with the Holy Spirit, Mary brought the Spirit to Elizabeth and to the unborn John, and we ask her to intercede with Christ that He may send His Spirit upon us.

Meditation for the Eighth Day

VIRGIN Mother of God, overflowing with mercy, have mercy on your child and undo this knot [mention your request here] in my life. I need your visit to my life like you visited Elizabeth. Bring me Jesus, bring me the Holy Spirit. Teach me to practice the virtues of courage, joyfulness, humility, and faith, and, like Elizabeth, to be filled with the Holy Spirit. Make me joyfully rest on your bosom, Mary. I consecrate myself to you as my mother, queen, and friend. I give you my heart and everything I have—my home and family, my material and spiritual goods. I am yours forever. Make my heart like yours, so that I can do everything Jesus tells me.

Mary, Undoer of Knots, pray for me.

Day 9

On the ninth day of the novena, we thank the Blessed Virgin for her intercession throughout this novena, which we hope will lead to our prayers being answered and the knots in our life being undone.

Meditation for the Ninth Day

MOST Holy Mary, our Advocate, Undoer of Knots, I come today to thank you for undoing this knot in my life. [Mention your request here]

You know very well the suffering it has caused me. Thank you for coming, Mother, with your long fingers of mercy to dry the tears in my eyes; you receive me in your arms and make it possible for me to receive once again the divine grace.

MARY, Undoer of Knots, dearest Mother, I thank you for undoing the knots in my life. Wrap me in your mantle of love, keep me under your protection, enlighten me with your peace! Amen.

Mary, Undoer of Knots, pray for me.

The reflections before each meditation were adapted from: https://www.thoughtco.com/mary-undoer-of-knots-novena-4010853.

LITANY OF TRUST[43]

From the belief that I have to earn Your love
Deliver me, Jesus.
From the fear that I am unlovable
Deliver me, Jesus.
From the false security that I have what it takes
Deliver me, Jesus.
From the fear that trusting You will leave me
more destitute
Deliver me, Jesus.
From all suspicion of Your words and promises
Deliver me, Jesus.
From the rebellion against childlike dependency
on You
Deliver me, Jesus.
From refusals and reluctances in accepting Your
will
Deliver me, Jesus.
From anxiety about the future
Deliver me, Jesus.
From resentment or excessive preoccupation
with the past
Deliver me, Jesus.
From restless self-seeking in the present
moment
Deliver me, Jesus.

From disbelief in Your love and presence
Deliver me, Jesus.
From the fear of being asked to give more than
    I have
Deliver me, Jesus.
From the belief that my life has no meaning or
    worth
Deliver me, Jesus.
From the fear of what love demands
Deliver me, Jesus.
From discouragement
Deliver me, Jesus.

That You are continually holding me sustaining
    me, loving me
Jesus, I trust in you.
That Your love goes deeper than my sins and
    failings, and transforms me
Jesus, I trust in you.
That not knowing what tomorrow brings is an
    invitation to lean on You
Jesus, I trust in you.
That you are with me in my suffering
Jesus, I trust in you.
That my suffering, united to Your own, will bear
    fruit in this life and the next
Jesus, I trust in you.

That You will not leave me orphan, that You are
    present in Your Church
Jesus, I trust in you.
That Your plan is better than anything else
Jesus, I trust in you.
That You always hear me and in Your goodness
    always respond to me
Jesus, I trust in you.
That You give me the grace to accept forgiveness
    and to forgive others
Jesus, I trust in you.
That You give me all the strength I need for what
    is asked
Jesus, I trust in you.
That my life is a gift
Jesus, I trust in you.
That You will teach me to trust You
Jesus, I trust in you.
That You are my Lord and my God
Jesus, I trust in you.
That I am Your beloved one
Jesus, I trust in you.

NOTES

1 Homily at the Living History Farms, ©1979, Libreria Editrice Vaticana.

2 *The Story of a Soul* (New York: Doubleday, 1957), p. 136.

3 According to tradition, St. Gertrude was told by Our Lord that each time she piously recited it, this prayer would release one thousand souls (or a vast number) from their suffering in purgatory.

4 *The Lamb's Supper: The Mass as Heaven on Earth* (New York: Doubleday, 1999), pp. 5, 128.

5 *The Imitation of Christ*, chapter 104.

6 Adapted from leaflet "My Day . . . A Mass" (Quebec: Au Service de la Vocation, 1966).

7 Ibid.

8 *God is Near Us* (San Francisco: Ignatius Press, 2003), p. 81.

9 Adapted from Pope Benedict XVI, Corpus Christi Homily, May, 2005.

10 From an "Act of Love to the Sacred Heart."

11   Fr. Lawrence G. Lovasik, SVD, *Communion Prayers* (Tarentum, PA), p. 12.

12   Ibid., p. 1.

13   Ibid., p. 2.

14   Ibid., p. 3.

15   Adapted from Lovasik, p. 4.

16   Adapted from "Prayer from an Eleventh-Century Manuscript of Winchester" in F. A. Gasquet, ed., *Ancestral Prayers* (Springfield, IL: Templegate Publishers, 1996), pp. 58–60.

17   Adapted from a prayer attributed to Father Cayetano de San Juan Bautista, http://www.josemariaescriva.info/article/opus-dei-founder-spiritual-communion-a-prayer-that-went-round-the-world.

18   A post-Communion prayer based on the teachings of Pope Saint John Paul II.

19   Excerpted from Lovasik, pp. 35–36.

20   Adapted from "Act of Thanksgiving," *The Key of Heaven* (New York, 1884), pp. 280–84.

21   Lovasik, pp. 34, 36.

22   Excerpted from Lovasik, p. 35.

23   This simple Marian prayer was clearly one of Mother Teresa's favorite prayers, as evidenced by the many variations of it that she would often recite or recommend to people.

24 "Our Lady of the Most Blessed Sacrament"
    https://yenra.com/catholic/prayers/be-
    forecommunion.html.

25 Excerpted from "After Holy Communion,"
    Praying in the Presence of the Lord (Hunting-
    ton, IN: Our Sunday Visitor, 1999), p. 48.

26 From a prayer of Fr. Mateo Crawley-Boevey,
    SS.CC., Founder of the Enthronement of
    the Sacred Heart. http://www.sscc.org/x_
    frames/homepage.

27 As cited by Fr. Stefano M. Manelli, FI, *Jesus
    Our Eucharistic Love*, pp. 50–51.

28 *Summa Theologiae* III, q. 80, art. 11, reply.

29 As cited by Fr. Stefano M. Manelli, FI, *Jesus
    Our Eucharistic Love*, p. 51.

30 From a pamphlet published by Msgr. M. J.
    Doyle, Toledo, OH.

31 *God Is Near Us*, pp. 97, 102–3.

32 Ibid., p. 93.

33 Lovasik, p. 31.

34 Adapted from the Divine Office, Prayer
    after the Psalm, Morning Prayer, Sunday
    of Week I, and from Divine Office, closing
    prayer of Morning Prayer, Week I.

35 *Prayers of Life* (Gill & Macmillan, 1965).

36 Excerpted from Lovasik, p. 8.

37 Based on the message of Pope St. John Paul
    II, August 15, 1996.

38   *Reflections and Prayers for Visits with our Eucharistic Lord* (Daughters of St. Paul, 1971).

39   Excerpted from "A Visit During the Day," *Praying in the Presence of the Lord*, pp. 65–66.

40   From "Prayer before Leaving for Apostolate," *Works of Love are Works of Peace: Mother Teresa of Calcutta and the Missionaries of Charity* (San Francisco: Ignatius Press, 1996), p. 203.

41   *Praying in the Presence of the Lord*, pp. 63–64.

42   As cited by Robert Cardinal Sarah, *The Power of Silence* (San Francisco: Ignatius Press, 2017), pp. 17–19.

43   Written by Sr. Faustina Maria Pia, Sister of Life. Used by permission, Sisters of Life, www.sistersoflife.org.